GIVE YOURSELF A

THE MINDSET AND MATH YOU NEED TO GET TO YOUR FIRST MILLION

Erin B. Haag

Give Yourself a Raise / Erin B. Haag —1st ed.

Paperback: 978-1-956989-21-2
Hardcover: 978-1-956989-22-9

DEDICATION

Dedicated to my two girls. You are kind, smart, strong, and brave. And you are good at math.

Contents

Introduction

It was June 17, 2015. I woke up at 5 a.m. to the sound of my crying infant. It was feeding time. I dragged myself out of bed, stumbled into her room, and began the usual routine. But something wasn't right. My neck was incredibly stiff, and I had a pounding headache. I thought maybe I had slept wrong and pinched a nerve in my neck. I rocked the baby and hoped the pain would disappear on its own.

After returning my daughter to her crib with a full belly, I crawled back into bed, hoping to capture an extra hour of sleep. Sleep eluded me. I couldn't relax because my mind kept racing through everything I had to get done that day. Take the girls to daycare. Rush into the studio. Teach clients. Manage the business. Answer a million emails. Pick up the girls and whisk them to their swim lesson. Whip together something edible for dinner. Bath. Storytime. Then bed. My head throbbed violently. "If this pain persists," I wondered, "how will I get everything done?"

Persist, it did! I tried to ignore the pain and push through the day—something I'd done time and time again in the past—but this time was different. I could not do it. Within a few hours, the hospital admitted me, and the diagnosis came quickly: viral meningitis.

Suppose you've never had the pleasure of experiencing meningitis. In that case, it's an inflammation of the brain and spinal cord that can lead to fever, chills, vomiting, a horrendous headache, and the kind of fatigue that makes you feel flattened by a truck. Not my idea of a good time! Your brain becomes so swollen that it actually touches the inside of your skull. The pain is so intense that no painkiller, not even morphine, can reduce it. Despite hearing all this from the hospital staff, I was still in denial. I felt certain I could spring back to my feet in no time.

"Your immune system is pretty low. Considering your stress level..." the neurologist informed me.

"Stressed? I'm not stressed," I interjected.

Almost immediately, the neurologist said, "You own a business, you have two babies under the age of two, and you're still recovering from the kidney infection you had two months ago."

Oh right. I neglected to mention that I had been admitted to this same hospital two months prior with a kidney stone that turned into an agonizing infection.

The neurologist finished: "Considering your stress level, it's no wonder the viral infection crossed the blood/brain barrier."

I remained silent as the cocktail of antiviral meds continued to drip into my veins.

Okay. So maybe I was a little stressed.

I was the owner and founder of a well-established Pilates studio—and full-time teacher trainer and regional director for an internationally recognized Pilates certification program. Despite increasing revenue at my studio year after year, payroll was always tight, profits were non-existent, cash flow was unpredictable, and I was working more and more (sometimes even 50 hours per week) while paying myself less and less. And did I mention the two babies at home?

I laid in that hospital bed for four days—followed by two weeks recovering on the couch at home. Even though my body was screaming for rest, the studio never left my mind.

I was convinced, "If I am not there, the business will suffer. I need to get back into the studio." But my suffering body wasn't well enough to tend to my suffering business. My doctor insisted that I recuperate and stay away from work.

Sprawled out on my back, all I could think was, "How did I get into this situation? I'm smart. I work hard. So, how come I never have enough money—and why do I feel so exhausted? What have I been doing wrong?"

Here's the thing about being forced to do bed rest. It gives you a lot of time to think. I reviewed the last several years in my head, trying to identify what, exactly, had caused my business (and life) to get into such an extreme state of distress.

Was the issue my branding, my marketing plan, my leadership style, my team? No. None of that. So then, what? As I evaluated my business, everything ultimately came back to one glaring issue: pricing.

The simple fact was that my prices were too low, and my pricing model set me up for failure. There was no way around it. The math does not lie. I was not charging enough to cover my business expenses, pay myself, and generate a profit, and I had zero predictable revenue. Most months, even when clients would pack into the studio, I was barely breaking even. That was the moment I realized that something needed to change—and that something was my pricing.

I had enough humility to recognize, "I need help," so I enlisted the help of a business consultant and began the process of restructuring my pricing model.

Seeking help was profoundly uncomfortable. I had to confront so many of my business-killing decisions and quickly realized, "My business is not set up for sustainability. The way I've been doing things is not working. I can't go on this way."

I felt guilt, shame, anger, frustration—every emotion imaginable—including fear. I kept thinking, "If I raise my prices, my clients will quit and go to another studio." "People will be so upset." "They won't like these changes that I need to make." I was afraid to change my business, even though I knew the current model was not working. I had to remind myself daily, "Set your emotions aside and trust the process." Ultimately, I rolled out a new pricing model, increased my prices, and announced the news to my clientele. It was a complete overhaul!

Once the pricing overhaul was complete, the business I once owned was no longer. What revealed itself in its place was a studio that operated seamlessly, generated predictable revenue, provided my staff and me with steady income, and turned a significant profit.

Three years later, almost to the day of my hospital stay, I sold my business for 40 times my original investment, debt free, with 100% of the sale proceeds going directly into my pocket.

All thanks to one (unwelcome) comment by a neurologist and the absolute power of math.

After selling the Pilates studio, it was time for a new chapter. I knew, "I want to help other women do what I did—overhaul their pricing and change their life."

I saw so many self-employed women suffering needlessly—caught in a cycle of undercharging and overworking. Smart, accomplished women barely making ends meet, earning just enough to survive or getting deeper into debt. In almost every scenario, the root issue wasn't the quality of their services. It was their pricing.

Over the next several years, I fine-tuned a specific process on how to evaluate your current business model and pricing, calculate the new pricing you need to start charging, and roll it out to your clients successfully. I call my approach: Pricing Overhaul®.

I made it my mission to end the madness and give women the tools they need to generate a profit—and have the life they want and deserve.

PRICING OVERHAUL®

Today, I run a coaching business called Pricing Overhaul®. The majority of my clients are self-employed women in service professions—think massage therapist, yoga teacher, dermatologist, gym owner, spa owner, numerologist, designer, copywriter, bookkeeper, coach, attorney—and here's what these women share in common.

They're excellent at what they do.

They are passionate about helping their clients achieve results, but they are working too many hours per week and not making enough money.

I work with each client to do a complete pricing overhaul. Upon finishing the process, my client has not only raised her prices (significantly), but she also has an upgraded business model—new premium offers with a premium price tag, new recurring revenue flowing in every month, and a whole new attitude about business.

Like I said. Complete overhaul.

THE WEIRD GIRL WHO LOVES MATH

While I never intended to become a pricing advisor, looking back, it all makes sense that I ended up in this career. Math has always come easily to me. One of my earliest memories from childhood was being "the weird girl who loves math" at my elementary school. There I was, sitting in my first-grade classroom, boiling over in frustration because my fellow classmates could not understand the simple math problem on the chalkboard—and I couldn't comprehend what was so difficult.

It wasn't until I stepped into the "real world" that I realized that most people don't think the way I do. I see the world in numbers. I solve problems very mathematically. It took me decades to recognize that I could use this natural ability to help women overhaul their businesses.

LAY OFF TO ENTREPRENEUR

Since graduating from college, I've spent 20 years working intimately with numbers, metrics, and pricing for large corporations and small privately owned businesses—not just with my Pilates studio.

Before starting my Pilates business in 2009, I held some significant roles in corporate America. Area supervisor, corporate sales trainer, call center manager, and even a QVC spokesperson. This gave me a deep understanding of business math and metrics. So it was no surprise when, in 2008, my corporate job laid me off due to the recession, and I decided to go into business for myself.

But here's the thing. Despite my natural aptitude for math and years of experience in corporate America, I made terrible decisions when it came to running my own business.

My emotional investment in my Pilates studio encouraged pricing decisions based on feelings, hopes, wishes, or fear—not based on math. This decision-making method led to a business in very poor shape, extremely high stress levels, and that fun bout of viral meningitis.

My point is that even if you're a brilliant woman, you can make very dumb pricing and business decisions. It happened to me. It can happen to anyone. But once you have a process to follow and you understand how to do the math, you start making vastly better decisions. That's what I will teach you to do in this book.

WHAT YOU'LL FIND IN THIS BOOK

I understand that just mentioning the words "math" and "numbers" might have you ready to run screaming into the night. But I am here to tell you that this journey will be easier than you think. This is my zone of genius. I make this process so easy to understand that even the most math-averse lady can walk away feeling like a badass math ninja—and with a profitable pricing strategy to prove it!

Here's what we're going to cover.

In *Part One: Shift Your Mindset*, we will address the mindset issues that keep women trapped in a cycle of undercharging and underearning.

Why do you undervalue your services? Why do you undercut your prices?

Why do you base pricing decisions on emotion, guessing, or copying a competitor—rather than actual math?

Why do you ask your husband, dad, or another male figure to make financial decisions on your behalf—rather than handling the numbers yourself? All of these choices stem from a particular belief system: that you are not good at math, that you are terrible with money, and that you cannot handle these matters successfully. All of this is false. To overhaul your pricing and business, we must first overhaul your mind.

We'll discuss where these damaging beliefs about money and pricing come from—and why they're so prevalent in our society. I'll teach you how to tell your inner critic to "shut the fuck up," a phrase my clients and I adore and use all the time. (It's cathartic to say shut the fuck up to that inner negative voice. Say it quietly—or loudly if the kids aren't around. Shut the fuck up!!! Doesn't it feel so good?)

In *Part Two: Overhaul Your Pricing*, we will DO SOME MATH! This is the fun part. I can sense you rolling your eyes at me right now, but trust me. The math is so exciting—especially when the numbers reveal your dream life and business.

I'll teach you how to plug numbers into simple spreadsheets (which I'll provide for you) to evaluate your current profit margin, calculate your monthly break-even, your monthly revenue needed (with profit baked in), your capacity for clients, your monthly client usage, your monthly client value, and other numbers you need to know. If you have no idea what those phrases mean, fear not—I will explain everything in plain English.

By the end of *Part Two: Overhaul Your Pricing*, you will have a new, upgraded menu of services that you're excited to roll out to your clients—with new, upgraded pricing to match. You'll have a new pricing model that enables you to run a high-profit business, work less, and earn more—while providing a premium experience to the people you serve. It's like a business makeover. Major improvement. This overhaul is a win not just for you but for your clients too.

And if you are wondering, "But how do I announce these business changes and higher pricing to my clients—without upsetting them?" Don't worry, because I cover how to do this too.

To become a premium service provider with premium pricing, you must step into a new chapter of life. You are becoming a new and better version of yourself—not just at work but in all areas of life. In *Part Three: Change Your Life*, we'll discuss how to embody this new version of you fully. Old behaviors you may have done in the past (paying an invoice late, haggling to get a discount, ordering the cheapest wine on the menu) is over and done, and you're not living that way anymore!

If you want to attract dream clients who respect you as a business owner, then you need to carry yourself differently through the world. Through your thoughts, actions, purchasing decisions, attire, and even your posture, you need to show the world, "I am a woman who delivers excellence to my clients. I get paid well. I hold unwavering and firm in my decisions. And I inspire others to do the same."

By the end of this book, you will know exactly how much you need to charge. You will feel more than worthy of the money you desire. And you will be unstoppable in all of your business endeavors.

IT'S TIME FOR A MAJOR OVERHAUL

In the United States, women entrepreneurs typically earn 28% less than their male colleagues. Over the full span of your career, this adds up to millions in lost earnings that could have been yours. In addition to the economic and social structures that favor men, one of the main reasons women underearn is that we undercharge. Plain and simple. Change your pricing, and you change your life. Once you overhaul your pricing, this is what happens…

You find yourself in a position where you can work 40 weeks a year instead of 52—and earn the same amount (or more) as before.

You can stop working five to seven days a week and shift to a four-day workweek—a reasonable schedule where you can breathe again.

You can become known as the premium provider in your industry—the top service professional, the go-to expert to hire, the best of the best.

Instead of earning just enough to eke by into the next month, you have surplus cash to invest back into your family, your health, and the things that bring you the most joy.

This is all within your grasp. You can have this kind of life. But you have to be willing to overhaul your prices. This is a step you must take. There is no getting around it. Doing this is not optional. And I'm going to help you do it.

By reading this book, you're taking a powerful step toward the income and life you truly want.

It's time to give yourself a raise—and get the mindset and math you need to get to your first million.

Let the overhaul begin.

PART ONE

Shift Your Mindset

CHAPTER 1:
You Are Good at Math

I want to begin with a very important message. Consider this a public service announcement from one woman to another. If I could put this message on a giant billboard in the center of Times Square in New York City—so millions of women see it daily—I would.

YOU ARE GOOD AT MATH.

I know. I know. You're reading this right now, shaking your head at me, thinking, "I'm sure you say that to everyone, but seriously Erin, you don't know me. I'm terrible at math."

I'm here to tell you: YOU ARE GOOD AT MATH!

Whenever I start working with a new client, one of the first things she says to me is, "I suck at numbers. Math stresses me out. I've never been good at it."

I look her directly in the eyes and say, "Can I be blunt with you?" and wait for the approval nod before I continue. "Every time there's a voice in your head that says, 'I suck at numbers', I want you to do one very important thing."

"And what's that?"

"I want you to tell yourself to shut the fuck up."

Her jaw drops to the floor, and her eyes bug wide open in disbelief as she processes this information.

"Talk back to that voice in your head and say *shut the fuck up!* Because those four words—'I suck at numbers'—are no longer allowed inside your head. That statement is a complete lie. And if somebody were lying straight to your face or insulting your intelligence, you would tell them to shut the fuck up… would you not?"

She trepidatiously commits to this assignment and nervously chuckles, "Okay, okay, I promise I will tell myself to shut the fuck up."

By the time our work together is finished and about a million "shut the fuck ups" later, she is a completely different woman.

She's tracking her numbers daily and updating her spreadsheets weekly. Keeping a close eye on her metrics. Oh, and she's raking in the money!

Why, then, does every single client initially think she's bad at math when clearly she is NOT? And why do women allow this false narrative to keep them trapped in terrible financial situations?

Conditioning leads us to believe that women are naturally bad at math and numbers. This belief is absolutely wrong. And you don't have to take my word for it. There is solid science to back this up.

According to a study conducted by researchers at Carnegie Mellon University, there are no gender differences in math ability between boys and girls. None. (Cantlon, 2019)

In fact, boys and girls have similar abilities regardless of age and brain maturity, meaning that a six-year-old girl is just as capable of doing math as a six-year-old boy. The same holds true for her entire life—when she's 25, 40, or 65—it doesn't matter the age. There are no differences.

Scientists have even used MRIs to scan the brains of both boys and girls when presented with math-related games and education. And guess what? The brain scans are identical. There is nothing about the male brain that inherently makes it better suited to doing math. Imagine that!

So, back to my original question: Why are so many women convinced that they are bad at math?

It's because society has conditioned us to believe that we are bad at math. Messages from teachers, parents, television shows, commercials, and other media sources gradually shape your attitude and cause you to think, "I guess I'm just not very good at this."

Throughout history, there have been many instances when everyone believed that something was true—only to discover, much later, that the exact opposite was true.

At one point, many believed (with absolute certainty) that the world was flat. We've since realized this isn't true at all. At another point in history, doctors believed smoking was good for you. Ads from the 1930s to 1950s would often depict a physician in a white lab coat encouraging you to: "Give your throat a vacation. Smoke a fresh cigarette." (Klara, 2015) It turns out that smoking is not good for your health. Duh! This seems obvious now. But clearly, it wasn't obvious back then.

It's the same scenario with women and math. We're still living in an era where millions mistakenly believe that women are less skilled with numbers—even though this is a complete lie.

Now, here's what is true.

Girls are statistically given less attention by teachers than their male counterparts in areas of science, technology, engineering, and math. Girls are encouraged to excel in other areas, such as reading, social studies, and art. Furthermore, parents tend to spend less time playing games with their daughters that involve spatial cognition—a skill that further develops math ability— than they play with their sons. Girls pick up on these societal cues and focus their attention on other subjects and interests, all while concluding to themselves, "I must be bad at math."

Take it from Shelley Correll, professor of sociology at Stanford University, who declared, "Boys do not pursue mathematical activities at a higher rate than girls because they are better at mathematics. They do so, at least in part, because they think they are better."

"Think" is the key word here. Men think they are better at math, even though this is not necessarily true. Women think they are worse, even when this isn't the case.

If you're still unconvinced that women are just as good at math as men—if not better—allow me to convince you, once and for all, thoroughly.

Statistically, women are reluctant to begin investing their money and wait until they are much older (compared to men) to begin investing. But according to the Fidelity 2021 Women and Investing Study, once women take the leap and start investing, they tend to outperform their male counterparts by 40 points per year.

Numerous studies, including one from researcher David Reilly, a member of the American Psychological Association, show that when it comes to taking tests—such as a math test or standardized intelligence test—overall, men and women tend to score about the same. However, their perception of their scores is very different. Men tend to overestimate their scores. Go figure—men overestimating the measurement of something. Women tend to underestimate. To paraphrase Reilly, men think they're brighter, and women think they're stupider than they actually are. (Reilly, 2022)

And this study will blow your mind—and hopefully shift your attitude forevermore. In a 1999 study led by Steven Spencer, published in *The Journal of Experimental Social Psychology*, researchers gathered together a group of men and women. They instructed them to take a math test. Prior to beginning the test, they told half the women, "We've noticed that women perform worse on this test compared to men." Guess what happened next? This group performed more poorly on the test. They told the other half of the women participants, "We've noticed that women and men perform equally on this test." And wouldn't you know it? This group performed equally. Solid proof that you are perfectly capable of doing math and there is nothing wrong with your brain. But when you receive disempowering messages from society—especially from people you respect and trust—it impacts your performance. (Spencer, 1999, 4-28)

In my profession, I see this science play out in everyday life with my clients, colleagues, and friends.

I once met a brilliant woman named Jennifer. She and I joined a mastermind group for women business owners. The members of this group are smart, accomplished, talented women who are each badasses in their fields. As the term "mastermind" suggests, we talk endlessly about our business goals. Of course, it should come as no surprise that I'm the resident math nerd in the group. I know. Shocker! My fellow masterminders often ask me about all things related to math, metrics, and pricing.

One time, Jennifer asked a question about her pricing—and immediately, I sensed anxiety rising in her chest when I gave her the mathematical formula to calculate her target price point. As I displayed the formula on my screen, I could see her facial muscles tightening, her cheeks flush, and her entire body seeming to cave in and contract. Her body language was saying, "I don't think I can handle this. I want to disappear."

As we continued to talk, Jennifer opened up about her anxiety surrounding math and numbers. She went on to explain that while she was never explicitly told "you are bad at math," she had decided this was true nonetheless.

She explained, "As a kid, my parents were often impatient with me when it was time to do my math homework."

When she didn't understand a problem, as many children do, she broke down into an "I don't get it" meltdown. Her parents would lose their cool (hello, fellow parents out there, haven't we all?), and sometimes they would scold her or even yell. She remembers the energy of their yells reverberating off her little body. Even though her parents never said, "You suck at math," their behavior sent a clear message to young Jennifer: "You are too slow. You are not good enough. You are not capable of doing this successfully."

Talk about heartbreaking.

Jennifer continued, "By age eight or nine, I had pretty much decided, 'I'm bad at math.'" Jennifer carried this attitude into adulthood, impacting her ability to run her business at the level she wanted. Like a stone dragging you down to the bottom of the sea, negative beliefs weigh you down heavily.

Today, Jennifer has a nine-year-old daughter of her own. Jennifer is noticing that her daughter seems to be struggling with math. One evening, when her daughter was grappling with her homework, Jennifer blurted out, "Mommy's not the best at math, so we're going to have Daddy step in and help you today."

And thus, this is how—as a society—we perpetuate the notion that boys are better at math and girls suck at it.

As Jennifer recounted this moment to me, she had an awakening. She realized, "I need to shift my mindset about this. If not for myself, then for my daughter's sake. I don't want her to grow up believing what I have believed."

"So," I asked her, "Are you really bad at math? Because you've shared with me that you love spreadsheets and use them regularly in your business. I would think that if you were bad at math, you wouldn't be able to input formulas into the spreadsheet cells."

"Well, the formulas I input into the spreadsheet cells are really simple," she said. "They're just adding, subtracting, and the occasional percentage calculations."

"Right. Pretty simple," I agreed. "But wouldn't you say that the formula I gave you to calculate your pricing is pretty simple, too? It's literally just adding and dividing."

"I guess I never thought of it that way," she said.

"Well," I challenged, "There's really no other way to think of it. The formula I gave you is nothing more than addition plus baking in a percentage. There's no reason to complicate it beyond that."

As if I had revealed the meaning of life, she cried out, "You're right. It is just that simple. I overcomplicated it in my head. OMG. I actually get it!"

In that moment, I could hear a lifetime of anxiety, stress, and insecurity melt out of Jennifer's voice.

Jennifer was never bad at math. She is perfectly capable of typing numbers into a spreadsheet and doing addition, subtraction, multiplication, and division with a calculator. She just made a (very wrong) decision about herself at a very young age. And I suspect you, my dear reader, have done the same.

Most likely, you've repeated the words "I am bad at math," "Math is hard," or "I'm not good at numbers" to yourself a thousand times. You've recited those words so many times, and at this point, you've deeply etched them into your psyche. You have convinced yourself that these words are true. They are not—and it's time to break the pattern.

Here are the new words I want you to say to yourself repeatedly. Do you know that song "New Rules" by Dua Lipa where she proclaims the rules on leaving a shitty relationship and treating yourself with dignity and respect? Well, these are your new rules for math. Say the following to yourself out loud:

I am good at math.

I am just as capable of doing math as a man.

I can absolutely type numbers into a spreadsheet and press "Enter" to find a result. This is not rocket science. This is easy.

Math can be simple. Add. Subtract. Multiply. Divide. No big deal. Just plug numbers into a calculator and boom! Done. There's no need to overcomplicate it.

I am excited to become a smart, sexy, confident math ninja.

Doing math is the path to creating my best business—and life.

Now that you've told yourself that you are good at math, the best way to shift your mindset is to do some math to prove to yourself, "I got this."

Here's what I want you to do.

Grab a calculator (the calculator app on your phone will do) and type in the following numbers:

1,007 x 10 and then press the equal (=) sign.

Did you get 10,070...? Great.

Now, do 10,070 divided by 5.

Did you get 2,014...? Good.

Now, do 2,014 x 200 and press equal. Then multiply that amount by 10.

Did you get 4,028,000...? Excellent.

Now take 4,028,000 and multiply times .25 (this means 25%). Press equal again.

Did you get 1,007,000...? You're doing it!

Lastly, take 1,007,000 and click the division symbol to divide by 1,000.

You should end up with the original number we started with: 1,007.

Got it?

Congratulations. You just did math.

If you successfully completed that assignment, then you can do everything else I teach you in this book. In fact, the rest of the math in this book is even easier because you just plug numbers into a spreadsheet that I provide—and the spreadsheet magically adds, subtracts, multiplies, and divides for you.

Despite what society may tell you, you do have the skills to overhaul your pricing and business.

You are good at so many things.

Including math.

CHAPTER 2:
You Can Manage Your Numbers

Like a horrible rash on your skin, one negative thought expands and leads to another. Before long, negativity covers you.

When you believe "I suck at math," this belief leads to thinking:

"I'm not very good at managing money."

"It's too overwhelming to look at the numbers."

"This isn't my strong suit. Isn't it better to focus on what I'm good at?"

"It would be better if I delegate all of the 'money stuff' to somebody else...."

Thus, the rash spreads.

Then you decide to delegate all of your business finances to somebody else who is, in your opinion, "good with numbers." Nine times out of ten, this person is either your husband, dad, or a male accountant (hello, patriarchy). This is exactly how the societal norm that "boys are better at math" gets perpetuated.

You give away your power when you don't manage your own business numbers.

Then, when it's time to make a decision about your business—for example, to purchase a new piece of equipment, hire a new team member, work with a coach, attend a conference, and so on—you must ask your husband, dad, or accountant whether or not you can afford to do it. Essentially, you must get permission from a man (insert eye roll) before making decisions for your own career and livelihood.

Let's pause for a moment to let the unpleasantness of that fact sink in!

More than half of women defer to men regarding financial decisions. This is true for women across the earning spectrum, from women who earn very little to those who earn a lot. According to *The New York Times*, the majority of high-earning millennial women defer to their husbands (or boyfriends) when it comes to financial matters. As one article states, "Even the most educated and high-achieving women do not participate equally with their husbands in long-term financial decision making." (Gross, 2020) What the actual F?

To quote journalist Cassie Werber, reporting for Quartz at Work: "When it comes to managing money long-term, wealthy women are opting out of responsibility and deferring to their male partners." (Werber, 2019)

What's especially disconcerting is the fact that younger women (ages 20 to 50) defer to their husbands most of all, more so than older women. You would think the younger generation would be busting out of these old societal norms, but that's not the case. If anything, we seem to be going backward.

When asked, "Why not take the lead and make financial decisions by yourself?" most women respond with, "Well, he knows more than I do."

He knows more? Oh no. Trust me. He does not. You simply assume that he does because that's what society has taught you to believe.

I've seen this scenario play out more times than I care to outline—across all age groups, financial brackets, and professions.

I've often hopped onto the phone with a prospective client who says, "Erin, I really want to work with you…" [lengthy, distressing pause] "…but my husband says I can't afford it."

Ladies, aren't we tired of asking men for permission?

I'll never forget the time I connected with a new client named Debbie. She and I had been chatting via social media about her fitness studio. She told me, "I love my fitness studio—it's my passion and life's work—but it's not generating a profit consistently. I need your help to turn things around."

"Let's do this," I told her and contacted her to set up an initial consultation. "What's a good date for us to meet?"

Well, Debbie insisted that we needed to work around her husband's schedule. She told me, "We have to find a time that works for him. He needs to be at the meeting too."

"Hmm," I thought to myself. "Why would her husband need to be on the call? Debbie owns this fitness studio, does she not?"

I want to preface this by saying Debbie's husband did not insist on attending the meeting—but being the incredibly supportive husband he is, he knew his wife lacked confidence when discussing her business numbers. So when asked, he was more than willing to shoulder that burden for her. And shoulder it he did for almost 10 years!

When I explained to Debbie that her husband did not need to attend the call, she dug in her heels and insisted.

"No. I won't do the call without him. He's the numbers guy. He knows all the numbers for the business, so it will be more productive if he's there. I won't be able to make any decisions without him, and I won't be able to explain our discussion to him afterward."

"Got it," I said, trying to sound courteous and cheery. But inside, my heart was sinking. I'd heard countless women—just like Debbie—say something along those lines a hundred times before. You would think we're living in the 1800s rather than the age of WiFi and recreational space travel.

And now I, a professional math expert, felt awkward and pressured to "perform" for Debbie's husband. I worried, "Will he assume that I can't do math?" I didn't know what to expect.

I prepared for our upcoming meeting more than I have ever prepared for anything in my life. You would have thought I was rehearsing to deliver a

TED Talk to millions. I felt anxious over whether or not this man would find me knowledgeable enough and whether he would ultimately give his blessing to allow his wife to hire me. The whole situation felt so awkward. I was determined to erase all possible doubts and prove I was more than qualified to help.

Prove myself I did. I flexed all my math muscles and put them on full display. At the end of the call, Debbie's husband (who, I want to note, was absolutely lovely, genuine, respectful, and kind) said, "Debbie, do it. I think this is what you need to do." I exhaled a major sigh of relief. Debbie officially enrolled as a client.

For our first few sessions, Debbie's husband joined us. (I want to add that Debbie is one of the lucky women who has a supportive husband who loves her endlessly and who wants nothing more than for his wife to succeed.) Over time, as Debbie's confidence grew, her husband became less and less involved. Eventually, all of our calls together were just Debbie and me.

I witnessed a complete and total transformation before my eyes, week after week. Debbie went from having no idea how much money her company was generating to a full-out Numbers Ninja. She arrived fully prepared for each meeting with her spreadsheets updated, her numbers tallied, and an eagerness to brag about her ever-increasing revenue!

Several months after we completed our work together, Debbie's business had skyrocketed, and she sent me a message that truly made my year.

It was a screenshot of a text message from her husband. After a particularly good month at her studio, he texted her to say:

"Where are you taking me to dinner, Profit Queen?"

Profit Queen! Just a few months prior, Debbie was too insecure to even attend a meeting without her husband in tow. She would bury her head in the sand and plead with him to handle things. But now, she's fully in charge. She knows all of her numbers. If you asked Debbie, "How much did your business generate in revenue last month? What were your business expenses?

What was your salary? How much did you set aside for taxes? What was your profit margin?" she could immediately whip out a spreadsheet and tell you all the details—with supreme confidence.

This is the transformation I love to see in my clients. (And I want you to experience it by the time you finish reading this book.)

It's the mindset shift from "I'm not good at managing money" to "I'm good at doing this—and it feels great to do it," "I know exactly what's going on with my business finances," I know what I can afford to do," and "I can make smart business decisions on my own—without needing to ask a man if it's okay."

Wouldn't it feel better to hold your power and authority—rather than give it to somebody else?

Repeat after me:

> *I am reclaiming my power.*
>
> *The only person who gives me permission is ME.*
>
> *Starting now, I will make all of the financial decisions in my business.*
>
> *The best person to run my business is me—the founder and business owner.*
>
> *I am ready to face the numbers and find out exactly how much money I am bringing in, spending, and keeping, and how to increase my profit margin. It's time.*
>
> *I am excited to manage my numbers and am more than capable of doing so.*

Here's what I want you to do before the end of today.

I want you to take back your financial power.

When your husband is considering investing in a particular stock or piece of real estate, you say to him, "I want to be part of this conversation. Let's look at the numbers together. Walk me through it."

This means that when you're thinking about investing in yourself or your company, you assess the situation and make that decision yourself. Your business. Your call.

If those steps feel too big right now, begin with a smaller step. Do something that represents you taking command of your money. This could be opening a new business savings account (that you intend to stuff full of cash—soon!) or putting a weekly appointment into your calendar to meet with a coach and review your latest numbers—without a man in attendance.

Take a step, big or small, that signifies "I'm taking charge."

You can manage your money and the numbers in your business perfectly. And, when you take full command of your business—rather than avoiding huge portions of it—your business becomes 10x stronger. The more you bring attention to your money, the more of it you will have.

CHAPTER 3:
You Are So Much More Than Your Numbers

We've all heard the saying, "It's going to get worse before it gets better."

That phrase brings me back to the days when acne covered my face. My dermatologist told me, "I'm going to prescribe a new treatment protocol. You need to understand that this will make your current acne worse. That part is temporary. Once the treatment starts kicking in, your skin will eventually clear up."

It's the same when it comes to your money.

Once you finally confront the numbers, it can be extremely uncomfortable. Looking at the math closely—and realizing that your business is in pretty bad shape—is not a fun moment. It can dredge up all kinds of emotions.

You may think, "I'm so embarrassed," "I am so stupid," "How did I let this happen?", "I'm so ashamed," "There's no way out," or "I'm not capable of running an actual business."

I always remind my clients, "The first part is the worst part. This moment might be painful, and it can feel so damn personal. But just like my acne-prone skin, it's going to get better."

If you've been neglecting your business finances for a while, chances are you're in for a rude awakening. You might sit down with a pricing advisor—or by yourself—and realize, "Whoa. My business is not profitable. I'm barely breaking even." Or, "I have a negative net worth. I'm in so much debt."

At that moment, your body may start reacting. You might feel heavy, dizzy, flushed, or shaky, or notice your heart beating faster. This is a stress response.

Take a deep breath. Exhale deeply. And remember these words:

These are just numbers.

This is information about your business.

It's not information about you, your soul, or your value as a human being.

The numbers say absolutely nothing about who you are and what you are capable of doing.

The numbers simply say where you are starting. Not where you are going. Not where you will end up.

In addition, I want you to remember that this current situation is not entirely your fault. Nobody ever taught you how to choose the correct price for your services, manage your money, track your metrics, and analyze your numbers (unless you got an MBA degree). You never learned how to do this.

If you're like most business owners, you opened your business because you are passionate about helping others, and you have a unique talent and gift to share with the world. You're likely the best at what you do, a true artist of your craft, and so you thought your talent and gift would be enough to turn into a profitable business. But then shit got hard, and you realized that talent alone wouldn't make you money. "This 'running a business thing' is hard as fuck," you thought. Of course, it is incredibly difficult if you never learned how to run a profitable business. If nobody ever taught you how to drive a car, then driving would be extremely difficult! It's the same with your business.

On top of that, you grew up in a society that continually hammers the message, "Women aren't good at math." Put it all together—lack of education, negative societal messages, shame, overwhelm—and you've got a perfect storm. No wonder this has been hard for you!

Here's one more thing I want you to remember:

It's going to get better from this point forward.

It really is. First, you need to learn how to separate your self-worth from your business numbers. These are not the same. Once you recognize you are valuable, this mindset shift allows you to earn more.

At my company, Pricing Overhaul®, one of my programs is called Once Upon A Profit. One client, Aaron, knew that she needed to join.

"I definitely need this," she wrote to me via DM. "But what worries me is, what if I just don't get it? I've never been good at understanding math. Will this program go way over my head?"

"Oh, don't worry about that. I make it super easy and fun!" I reassured her. "And if you have any questions, that's what I'm here for."

"Yes! You do make it fun! But my money is such a mess. I have no idea how much revenue I earn each month or my business expenses. I don't even have a business checking account. I just do everything using my personal account. It's a hot mess…" she went on.

"Everyone feels that way when they begin the program," I assured her. "You'll be in good company. Together, we can work on cleaning up that mess."

Aaron mulled it over but didn't sign up for the program. Something held her back.

A bit later, she wrote to me again. This time, she revealed something she hadn't shared before.

Aaron felt deep, intense shame.

"I've been so ashamed about my financial situation. I literally cry from embarrassment," she admitted. "I've never asked anyone for help."

Initially, Aaron told me, "I'm just not good at understanding math." A common belief. But later, the real truth came out: "I am ashamed at how bad my situation has become." She was scared to look at her business finances more closely because she worried, "What do these numbers say about me—as a person?"

As a woman, you might wrap your self-worth into your business. If your business is doing well, you figure, "I must be smart." If your business is not doing so well, well then you assume, "I must be a worthless piece of poop." And let's be honest, none of us want to look in the mirror to see a piece of poop staring back at us.

I knew what Aaron needed to hear.

"As women, managing our money isn't something we are taught," I informed her. "And then we feel ashamed that we don't know how to do it. Can you see how unfair that is?"

I went on, "This shame keeps women from actually trying to manage their money because it's easier to hide behind the old 'I'm just not good at this' narrative than it is to admit that we haven't received the necessary tools."

"So true," she declared. "I'm literally tearing up as we talk! This is monumental for me. I have never asked for help! I've been limping along for the past 22 years with my business. I'm ready to face the numbers."

Getting into your numbers for the first time is like cleaning out your closet. Oh dear God, just the thought of it makes you sweat. You know it's going to be uncomfortable. You know it's going to take all damn day. You know you are going to face triggering feelings. Some items will flood you with memories that make you cry. Others you'll identify as "crap" and decide to toss. A few select items will be treasures that you keep and reorganize. But once you clean out the closet, you know it will feel so good. Then, you'll look forward to opening the closet doors—knowing that nothing will topple off the highest shelf and smack you on the head.

Eleven days later—after a deep dive into the current state of her business numbers—I received this message from Aaron:

"Thank you soooooo much! I already feel so much better. I'm actually excited about numbers, math, where I'm at, and where I am going. Having you by my side, guiding me, gives me so much confidence and makes this journey way less scary! Take that in your pipe and smoke it, Money Fear!!! I'm going to make you my BITCH!"

Pure poetry! Music to my ears! Smoke that, indeed!

Talk about a total transformation.

Just like Aaron, you may be feeling completely overwhelmed by the prospect of "facing the numbers." The notion of logging into your bank account, checking your credit card balance, digging into that tragic shoebox stuffed with receipts, or looking at a spreadsheet might cause you to break out in hives.

The reason it feels so scary is that you're connecting your self-worth to the numbers. Your mindset is, "If I am financially disorganized or not earning enough money, this means I am a bad person. I am a failure. I don't deserve to be liked, loved, or respected. Shame on me." This is simply not true.

I want you to consider all the factors that make you a great person. You're a caring daughter, sister, and niece. You help out your friends when they're in need. You would do anything to protect your children. You care deeply about your clients and do everything within your power to serve them well. You are the best in your industry. You have superpowers—perhaps you're an incredible teacher, hilarious storyteller, and writer, or you have a knack for making spaces look magazine-quality beautiful—and you generously share these superpowers with the world! You have contended with challenges in the past, and you're still kicking. You were courageous enough to go into business for yourself, something many people dream about but never do. And you have inherent value simply by being alive.

You are not a bad person. You are an excellent, remarkable person who needs help regarding numbers and money inside your business. You simply need to fill gaps in your knowledge.

As I said earlier, your current business numbers do not say *anything* about you as a human being. Whether cell A14 on a spreadsheet says $432 or $56,788 or -$13, this is mathematical information. It's not a reflection of your intelligence.

You could be the smartest person on earth—a MENSA-level genius—but if nobody ever taught you how to steer a sailboat or bake a croissant, then you wouldn't know the process and you would struggle. You would crash that boat or scorch that dough in the oven—something I have done countless times, as my daughters can attest, because I never learned how to bake! Hence: a kitchen filled with black smoke! Disaster! Same with your business. Nobody ever taught you the systems for success, which is why you have floundered in the past. All of that changes now. You are officially learning how to price your services correctly and manage your money well. This means your future will be very different from where you've been.

Repeat after me:

I am ready to face the numbers.

I am more than my numbers.

The numbers don't define me.

The only place to go from here is UP!

"When you know better, you do better," says Maya Angelou.

I am NOT a piece of poop.

I am a powerful, badass woman.

I have done hard things in my life and survived and thrived.

This process is going to be uncomfortable. Think childbirth. Labor can be excruciating, but holding your baby in your arms makes it all worth it. You are strong enough to handle the tough parts and the pay-off is enormous.

You can do this.

I want you to imagine that I'm sitting right by your side—pouring you a glass of wine (or maybe two), patting your shoulder, squeezing your hand, and reminding you, "You got this."

Even if you log into your online banking and discover that you have $2 to your name—dude, I've been there—and $50,000,000 in debt, this information is not going to kill you. This is not the end of your story. Those numbers do not spell out what your life is going to be like forevermore. Those numbers simply say, "This is where we're starting the journey." This is Point A. Point B is going to be a very different place.

To be a woman who's willing to confront a difficult situation and actually deal with it—what does that say about you? That says a lot about your character. To me, that says, "This is a woman on the rise. Get out of her f'ing way."

It might feel worse before it gets better. But it will get better, and that's for damn sure. The sooner you begin, the sooner you'll get to Point B.

CHAPTER 4:

You Can Charge More Than Your Competitors

Now that you're ready to come face-to-face with your numbers, it's time to get real about how much you can (and should) charge.

Let's begin here: How did you determine your current pricing?

If you currently sell a 90-minute massage for $90 or home decluttering services for $395 per day or wellness coaching priced at $1,995 for six weeks, how did you arrive at that decision?

If I had to guess, I would say you didn't choose your pricing based on math.

Instead, you randomly picked a number out of your butt and figured, "This will do!"

Or you did your own watered-down version of "market research." You looked around at what others were charging for similar services. Then you determined, "Welp, I guess this is an appropriate price. Let's go with that."

You may have even thought, "Everyone out there is more qualified than I am. They probably know more about pricing than I do. After all, so-and-so has been running a business for years. Whereas, I'm just starting out. So if she's charging XYZ, that must be a good price."

Wrong.

Here are the cold hard facts:

According to the Women's Business Enterprise National Council, only 12%

of woman-owned businesses generate $100,000 per year and above. 88% make less than $100,000. (WBENC, 2018)

This means the majority of women are undercharging, underearning, and struggling to make ends meet. If you bring 10 women business owners into a room, chances are, eight or nine of them are not earning as much as they want (or need) and feel financially stressed. Outward appearances do not always accurately reflect what's going on in one's bank account.

You might assume that everyone out there is smarter and wealthier than you are, but the statistics show that this is not the case. The majority of women entrepreneurs own and operate businesses that are barely profitable and that are unsustainable. This is why copying another woman's pricing is such a terrible move. You are copying a flawed model.

So, I'll ask again. How did you determine your pricing?

Did you look closely at your operating expenses, payroll, owner's compensation, taxes, and profit margin to determine exactly how much you need to charge?

Or did you copy your competitors, assuming they must have it all figured out? ('Cause they sure don't!)

I am here to tell you that your competitors did NOT do the math! Simply based on the sheer number of women I have worked with, I know this for a fact. Millions of women appear to run a "successful business" but are barely breaking even—not turning a healthy profit. They may have wonderful clients, excellent services, and an attractive website, but they're not paying themselves enough for their work. I make this claim with 100% certainty.

Most likely, your competitors did the exact same thing you did and copied their competitor's pricing. Because they also thought, "Everyone else must be smarter than me." Or they may have even undercut their competitor's pricing to gain what they believed would be a "competitive advantage" (please note the sarcastic quotation marks!).

Imagine this pattern of pricing playing out year after year, decade after decade, on repeat. When she's undercharging and you mimic her pricing, now you're undercharging too. Then, another woman comes along, sees your business, and bases her pricing off yours. The cycle of undercharging continues—and it's a race to the bottom.

This is one race you do not want to be leading!

There is only one way to set your pricing: math. Period. End of sentence.

I try to avoid generalizing based on gender. But there are certain things that we as women can learn from men—one of those is how they approach pricing.

Men usually don't think that other men are smarter than they are. Men don't copy other men's pricing. *Men just do the math.* They open a business. They know their expenses, their profit margin, and how much they will pay themselves. Then, they calculate how much they need to charge strictly based on the numbers. It's simple. No self-doubt. No emotional struggle. Just math.

You may argue back, "Okay, Erin. I see your point. But that still doesn't change the fact that so-and-so charges $90 for a massage and she seems really successful. So, that's what I should charge too. Right?"

Not right.

I repeat: Just because a competitor appears to be financially successful doesn't mean she actually is. You don't have all the information.

Unless you can get a good, hard look at her profit and loss statement—something I think you'll find nearly impossible to come by—there is no way for you to know for sure how successful she is. Sure, she might seem affluent and secure. Her business might look as though it's the hottest place on the block. But looks can be deceiving and often are.

Most likely, she's struggling financially—big time. Because (recall the statistic I mentioned earlier) *88% of women in business are struggling.*

She's probably generating just enough revenue to pay her expenses but not enough to pay herself an excellent salary. She's exhausted and heading for burnout. There is a very high likelihood that she is undercharging—because that is what most women do.

You might come back at me, proclaiming, "I can't charge more than my competitors do…" or "But everyone else in my area charges XYZ…".

I've heard these arguments one million times. And roughly half of those million came from my client Martine.

Martine began working with me post-pandemic. I knew immediately that this woman was one smart cookie—creative, smart, and resilient. She's a survivor and a hero. Despite numerous obstacles, she kept her business open during the COVID-19 crisis. Although the pandemic decimated millions of small businesses around the world, Martine managed to keep going. And she had the battle wounds to prove it.

After getting through 2020 and 2021, two incredibly difficult years in her business, Martine was ready to rebuild and reinvent. She enrolled in my signature program, which is called Pricing Overhaul®.

At first, Martine did not believe she had a pricing issue. She believed she needed to improve other aspects of her business—the client journey, sales conversion rate, and backend tech.

She told me, "I'm going to skip the part of the program that covers pricing. That part doesn't really apply to my situation. I'll do the other parts and then come back to pricing at the end if needed."

Alarm bells rang out in my head. I knew that Martine, despite her best intentions, was trying to skip the portion she needed most.

"It's best to start with the numbers," I explained. "We want to do this right from the start, rather than skipping ahead and then having to go backward."

"Hmmm, I get that..." Martine replied, although honestly, I did not entirely convince her.

One thing I've learned (from past mistakes) is to hold firm to your process. Do not yield. As an entrepreneur, when you have a proven process that works and you're the expert in this area, do not alter your method to appease a client. Because clients don't always know what they need—that's why they're coming to you for help. So, even when a client insists, "I don't really need to do that..." you need to gently assure them, "Oh, but you do."

I knew Martine had a pricing issue with her business—even if she wasn't ready to admit it. I firmly nudged her to do the math and look at the numbers.

Two weeks later, I received a message from Martine:

"Erin, I'm realizing you're right. I haven't increased my rates since January 2019—almost three years ago, at this point. It's time to revisit my pricing. I want to get really clear on what I need to charge and why."

Yahtzee! I was thrilled to help Martine overhaul her pricing to post-pandemic standards.

Our work began.

We analyzed all of her margins and crunched all of the numbers. And we ended up with significantly higher pricing than any of her competitors.

"Ugh." Martine was not exactly delighted. "These rates are much higher than anyone else in my area. For most of my clients, this is a 35% increase on their current rates."

"Yup," I nodded. "But we did the math, and these are the rates. This is what the math told us."

"I just don't think I can do it. Nobody else charges this much," she balked.

"I understand. But these are the prices you must charge in order to pay all of your expenses, pay yourself, and have a profit. You can choose to charge less, but in doing so, you're choosing the business and life you don't want," I encouraged.

Reluctantly, she agreed.

She made the price adjustments to her point of sale (POS) system. She prepared all of her new pricing sheets. She created phone scripts and email templates to make it easier to communicate the new pricing to clients. She had everything ready to roll out. Our work together positioned her finger to pull the trigger.

But then she second-guessed herself.

As doubt crept in, Martine sent me an audio message on Voxer, saying: "Hey, Erin. I spoke with a marketing consultant. We were talking about the new pricing plan. She agreed that this new pricing is too high. So, she and I came up with a different plan."

Hearing this message, I felt my heart sink. I could see precisely what was happening here. Martine was completely ready to roll out her new menu of premium services with a premium price tag—but got cold feet at the last second. So, she found a different "expert" who would "allow" her to charge less.

Martine tried to convince me that this "new direction" would be more successful—but I was not having it.

Now listen, I'm not knocking marketing consultants. There is value in knowing the trends in your industry, and what competitors are doing in your area, and learning creative ways to get more clients in the door. All of that is terrific. However, if a consultant tells you, "I did market research, and here's what your competitors are charging; therefore, that's what you should charge too…" turn and run in the other direction! Flee! As we've previously established, this is a flawed way to set pricing.

I explained this to Martine and begged her to trust the process. "The numbers never lie," I reminded her.

Martine contemplated the matter for a few more days. Eventually, she notified me, "Okay. I'm going to roll out the higher pricing like we previously discussed."

I exhaled a massive sigh of relief.

Thank goodness she trusted the process—because Martine's business went from a -8% (yes, negative) profit margin to a 21% margin three months later.

When Martine's program with me came to an end, she sent me the most incredible message:

"I feel really appreciative of all of the work we did and your advice through the pricing transition. I would not have done it without your support. It's giving me some space to breathe now that the numbers are up."

Space to breathe.

That happens when you choose pricing based on what you need to charge and not what everyone else is already charging.

Someone in your industry needs to be brave enough to do the math and raise her rates. And that brave woman is YOU.

Repeat after me:

I don't need to mimic other women's pricing.

I don't need to follow what's perceived as "standard" for my industry.

I can set pricing that makes sense, math-wise, for my company.

I can become the premium provider in my field—with premium pricing to match.

I'm excited to become the best—and most expensive—option. I want to be a high-end provider, not a cheapo discount option.

By raising my prices, I'm sending a message to my community—par-
ticularly fellow women business owners. Through my actions, I'm
demonstrating, "We've all been undercharging for too long. We all need
to charge more. And I'm going to lead the way."

We're long overdue for a financial revolution.

You can lead the charge (pun VERY much intended).

CHAPTER 5:

You Can Charge More Than Your Personal Budget Allows

You are not your client.

"Okay, where are you going with this, Erin?" you might be thinking. "Obviously, I am not my client. And your point is…?"

My point is that you might say things like this to yourself all the time:

"I can't charge my clients $250 for a massage. Personally, I would never be able to pay that much!"

"I can't charge $5,000 for a wellness retreat. I would never be able to afford something like that!"

"I can't charge $20,000 for a consulting package. That's not something I could realistically afford to do. And if I can't afford it, surely my clients can't either."

Again, I repeat:

You are not your client.

You, my friend, are a woman who decided to open a business to serve *others* using your gifts and talents. You invested time, energy, and probably a lot of money into learning and honing your craft. You invested blood, sweat, tears, coffee stains, and wine spills (presumably, even more money) into starting your business. You may have even gone into debt, taken out business loans, or relied on credit cards to get your business off the ground or keep your business afloat during difficult times.

So it's no surprise to me when you say, "I wouldn't be able to afford those high-end prices." No shit, Sherlock! Of course you can't afford those prices right now because you have sacrificed so much and you've depleted yourself trying to bring your business to this point. And because you're not charging enough.

You're barely struggling to get by month after month at your current rates. You're constantly worried about when the next sale will come in. You aren't able to pay yourself consistently. Forget about having discretionary income to invest in a deluxe massage, luxurious wellness retreat, or life-changing consulting services—the types of services that you might offer to your clientele.

It is possible that your own services are not within your own personal budget. You couldn't afford to hire yourself. This will continue to be your predicament—as long as you continue to undercharge. But this doesn't have to be your reality forever.

Here's the big message I want to impart to you in this chapter. Read these words. Circle them with a big yellow highlighter. Put this statement on a coffee mug, tattoo it on your arm, or stitch it onto a decorative throw pillow!

You cannot allow your personal financial situation to dictate how much you charge your clients.

Instead of thinking, "I can't charge XYZ—I could never afford a service like that!", or "Who would be able to afford that? Not me!", I want you to think: "I can't wait until I AM able to afford it."

Do you think the realtor selling the multimillion-dollar mansions on the beach could afford to buy her own mansion on the beach when she first started selling houses? Probably not. But that didn't stop her from selling multimillion-dollar homes to buyers who could. The more multimillion-dollar homes she sold, the more she made. The more she made, the closer she got to buying her own dazzling dream house on the beach, complete with an infinity pool, jacuzzi, and jaw-dropping ocean views.

But what if that realtor had said to herself, "There's no way I could afford to buy a multimillion home personally. So instead of selling high-end homes, I'm going to sell lower-priced homes because that's how much I could afford."

If that's the decision she made, here's how it would play out: She would sell low-end homes, get a low-end commission, and forever and always only be able to afford a low-end home herself.

Do you see the cycle here? When you choose pricing based on what you can afford, you keep yourself trapped in a loop you don't want to be in.

When you set pricing based on your own pocketbook, you attract clients with similar pockets—and without even realizing it, you turn away the clients who can (and will) pay higher prices.

Always remember *you are not the client.* The client is the client. Their financial reality may be very different from yours. And that is why you need to base your prices based on what? Math. Math and only math. Not based on emotion. Not based on what your peers are charging. Not based on what you imagine your client can pay. Based on math.

You need to crunch the numbers to find out what you must charge to create the profit margin you need. Whatever the math tells you, that is what you must do. Once you roll out this higher pricing, your dream clients—the ones who can happily pay this amount without any hesitation—will show up in your life. Now look, I know you're raising an eyebrow and going, "Oh, they're just going to show up, really? Just like that? Like magic? Forgive me if I'm not buying it."

Let me give you an example to prove my point.

I undercharged during the first five years I ran my Pilates studio. I priced my classes and private sessions at the exact same price as every other studio in my area (all of my competitors were undercharging too), and everything suffered for it—remember viral meningitis?

When I finally worked up the nerve to increase my prices, I remember thinking, "Who in the world could afford $120 for a private Pilates session?" My spreadsheet told me that $120 was what I needed to charge. I knew the math didn't lie. Even so, YIKES. $120 seemed like an awful lot.

"For most of my clients, that's going to be $1,440 per month," I calculated. At that time in my life, $1,440 was nearly the same as my mortgage payment on my townhouse. Would clients actually pay a *mortgage* for Pilates?

Here's what you don't know. I live in Palm Beach County, Florida, one of the country's wealthiest areas. The most affluent zip code in the county belongs to a little 7.803-square-mile island known as the Town of Palm Beach. We locals just refer to it as "The Island." Living on The Island—also dubbed Florida's Billionaire Hub—are 44 billionaires with a combined net worth of $61.6 billion. That is a vast amount of wealth, all sitting on one tiny stretch of Florida! To name just a few local residents: Jimmy Buffet (yes, the Margaritaville guy), Jon Bon Jovi (swoon), Rod Stewart (British rock icon), and Vera Wang (legendary fashion designer who creates couture gowns for celebs like Alicia Keys and Mariah Carey). Among the remaining 8,679 residents of The Island, the average annual household income is $328,465. For perspective, the average annual household income in the entire state of Florida is a little over $83,104, so it's more than fair to say that Palm Beach Islanders have serious money.

My studio just so happened to be located a few miles west of South Palm Beach Island, so it drew a large crowd of island residents. While the majority of my studio clients did not live on the island, they came from neighboring communities that were also on the higher end of the wealth spectrum.

Despite knowing how much wealth surrounded me, I remember holding my breath every time I quoted the monthly price for three private sessions per week. "Holy crap," I would think. "Are they going to balk at the $1,440 price tag? Are they going to spin right around and walk out the door and find another cheaper studio?"

Balk they did not. Nor did they spin! Why not? Because to these clients, $1,440 a month was not a mortgage payment. It was discretionary income they wanted to invest in Pilates for their personal well-being. These clients wanted to look and feel their best. They wanted a clear mind and toned core. They understood that consistently doing Pilates would upgrade their physical health—and mental health too. For them? This investment was 100% worth it.

"How nice it must be to have an extra $1,440 laying around each month to pay for Pilates," I thought to myself. "That is so distant from my current reality! But one day, I want to know what that's like!"

You know what?! Today, I do know what it's like—and let me tell you, it is absolutely delightful! I recently calculated that my husband and I spend a combined $2,635 per month on fitness and personal training because we can! Finally!

That breaks down to…

- $560 per week on six personal training sessions
- $220 per month for two separate gym memberships
- $175 per month for a sports nutrition tracker

And that doesn't even include the money we invest in regular chiropractic care, massages, meal preparation, etc.

My point is that Erin, who opened her studio at 27 years old, could not afford over $2,600 per month for exercise—let alone the $1,440 per month she eventually charged her clients. But 40-year-old Erin, who sold a profitable business and now owns a consulting firm that helps other women grow their profitability, sure as hell can!

But let's roll back in time to Erin on a budget. She faced a fork in the road. She had to decide, "Am I going to charge the lower prices I could personally afford? Or will I increase my prices based on what the math tells me I need to charge?" If I had chosen the first option, the story would have unfolded very differently. I would still be sitting on a tight pocketbook and would not be writing this book today.

"Okay, I hear what you're saying, Erin, but your clients actually had lots of money. Mine do not. There is no way my current clients can afford higher prices," you may be thinking.

Wrong!

Don't make assumptions about what your client can or can't afford. Unless they turned over their bank account username and password, access to their credit card statements and portfolio of investments, and copies of their last five to ten years' worth of tax returns, you don't know their personal financial situation.

Perhaps your client just got a massive divorce settlement and would love to spend some of that cash on a luxury wellness retreat—she could really use some TLC after months of agony. Or your client just got a tax refund and wants to invest back into her business by hiring an excellent designer. Perhaps your client owns her own business and just had the best month she's ever had since opening, and wants to celebrate with a pampering spa package. If you're going to make an assumption, assume this: "My client wants to hire the top provider in the industry, pay top dollar, and get premium results."

While the above scenarios sound great, not every client just received a windfall of money. I'll agree with you on that. Your client might be on a fixed income and only has a certain budget to invest in your services. But have you ever considered that maybe, just maybe, your services are so valuable to her that even if the prices increase outside of her current budget, she will find a way? People, especially women, always find a way. When it comes to getting something you really want, you will figure out a way to make it happen—and your clients will do the same.

Can you remember a time in your life when there was something you really wanted—but it was out of your budget? Did you still pull it off, nonetheless? Of course you did! Because you're a woman who decided, "This is more than I expected to pay, and it feels like a stretch, but I'm going to figure this out."

Then what did you do next? You came up with a side hustle to rake some extra cash in the door. You sold a used bike, treadmill, handbag, or coat. You redirected your spending—maybe you skipped something that felt like a low priority to preserve cash for something you wanted much more. You rented out a spare bedroom in your home. You asked your employer for a raise or bonus. People do these things all the time—and there is no reason your clients wouldn't do these things too. If a client truly wants to work with you, they will get creative and figure out a way to make it happen.

You may say to yourself, "I feel like I couldn't afford to pay XYZ." You may also say, "I feel like my clients can't pay that amount either." Both of these are feelings, not *facts*. You need to stick to the facts. What is the amount you need to charge to generate a healthy profit? That is what you *must* charge. This amount might be outside of your personal budget (for now, anyway), and that is okay. It's more than okay; it's actually a good sign! If you are charging more than you could personally afford, this means you are charging the amount that's going to bring your lifestyle to a higher level. You want to be the realtor selling multimillion-dollar beach homes—so that one day, you too, can afford a home like that or something close.

I want you to say the following statements out loud to yourself:

I am not my client.

My personal financial situation has nothing to do with how much I need to charge.

I will not make pricing decisions based on my own pocketbook.

My clients value my services and are willing to do what it takes to pay for them.

There are 7.9 billion people on the planet. That's a huge amount of people. There are dozens, hundreds, thousands, or even millions of people in the world who absolutely can afford my services.

I can't wait until I'm in a position where I can afford to hire someone like me.

I will get there eventually. And I'll get there a lot sooner if I increase my prices right now.

CHAPTER 6:

You Can Help Those in Need—and Earn a Great Living

"I started a business because I want to impact people's lives and make the world better. I'm here to serve."

"In order to be of service, I need to be accessible to everyone. If my prices are too high, I won't be accessible to everyone who needs me."

[long, pregnant pause…]

"Therefore, I should keep my prices low. That way, everyone will be able to afford me—even people who don't have much money."

Okay. Let me stop you right there, Mother Teresa. There are so many things about this line of thinking that absolutely drive me up a wall, but the biggest one for me is—and this is something I didn't learn until I became a parent—you do not need to make yourself accessible to everyone!

There. I said it. And I'm going to say it again (for impact) because this is vital to your health, well-being, and business sustainability.

YOU DO NOT NEED TO MAKE YOURSELF ACCESSIBLE TO EVERYONE!

When you make yourself accessible to everyone, you give and give until nothing is left for you to share. You run yourself ragged, trying to accommodate everyone else, sacrificing yourself in the process. You feel as though you can never say "no" or turn people away. Forgetting about your own needs, you put everyone else's needs first. Resentment builds and builds. Eventually, you reach a breaking point. You're no longer enjoying the work you used to love, and you realize, "I can't continue living this way. I need a massive change." That's when you burn down your entire business and start over from scratch. New logo! New brand! Pivot! Only to find yourself repeating the same patterns from the past—albeit under a new business name.

Or it plays out like this.

In an effort to be accessible to everyone, you undercharge severely and rarely (or never) turn a profit. Your stomach churns with anxiety every single month, wondering if you'll have enough money to pay the bills. You swipe your card at the grocery store and pray it doesn't get declined. You're unable to pay yourself what you need, let alone what you deserve, and eventually your choice to undercharge forces you to shut your business doors forever—because you can't afford to remain open.

Consider that. *Closing your business.* Is that helpful to anyone? Does that represent you following your calling and being of service? Is that your highest and greatest calling? No. Even the actual Mother Teresa would give you some serious side-eye and say, "Honey, going broke and shutting down your business is not the best way to serve humanity."

If you are accessible to everyone, you are of service to no one, especially yourself. If your fixation is on being accessible to everyone, you cannot serve your clients at the highest level for the long haul.

"Okay, I totally get that," you might be thinking, "but I offer a desperately needed service and I don't think it should be exclusively accessible to those with financial means. I want to make sure anyone who wants my services can have access."

Fantastic! I agree with you! Don't we all want to help people who might not normally have access to our services? Absolutely! And you can—but it doesn't require you to sacrifice your entire business and life to only serve those in need. That's what nonprofits do. Suppose you find yourself leaning more toward the nonprofit sector and less toward the for-profit sector; more power to you. But something tells me you picked up this book because you own a FOR-PROFIT business. By the very nature of owning a for-profit business, you need to make a profit.

"But I don't do this for the money" is something I commonly hear, to which I say, "Bullshit!" Unless you are sitting on a hefty trust fund, living on The Island of Palm Beach and don't need to take home an income, you are doing it for the money.

Everyone is doing it (at least partially) for the money. If you weren't doing it for the money, you wouldn't be doing it at all, or you'd be doing it for free as a volunteer. Although, at your current price points, it might feel like you're an overworked volunteer—because there isn't any money in your bank account! You might feel like an unpaid intern or volunteer in your own business, especially if you haven't paid yourself in a while. It is time to stop volunteering for your business. You deserve to get paid, and you deserve to get paid well.

Also, there is nothing wrong with doing it for the money! When people say, "I don't do it for the money" [smug smile, hair toss], it has such a condescending tone as if the people who are "doing it for the money" are somehow morally deficient. We all need money to keep a roof over our heads, put food on the table, and pay our bills. Needing money (or, gasp, dare I say it…*enjoying money*) doesn't make you a morally bankrupt person!

You should be able to pay for your kids' extracurricular activities, vacations, nice meals out, gifts for family and friends, retirement savings, a spa day for yourself, and anything else you desire. After all, this is why you opened a business in the first place. To make money doing something you love. And you know what? How lucky are you to have found a career you're so passionate about! You get to do something you love, positively impact the people you serve, and get paid to do it. Win *fucking* win!

This brings me to my next point.

You *can* help people in need *and* make money. You do not have to choose between one or the other. They are not mutually exclusive.

Once in a while, when I'm two glasses of Côtes du Rhône deep into the night and feeling bored, I peruse online forums and read through the posts from business owners. There, I find cringe-worthy comments that make me shake my fist at the sky and sigh heavily.

"I'm so tired of people in our industry only focusing on the money. It's not about the money. It's about helping people!"—Hailed as a martyr

"What about all the people who need our help? If I only cared about the money, then people who need my services wouldn't be able to get them."—Canonized as a saint

"I am doing this to serve people. To serve, I must charge less."—Falls on sword

I understand that these business owners have good intentions. However, I want to shake some sense into these people because these comments perpetuate the idea that you must sacrifice your own personal financial security to help people.

This couldn't be further from the truth.

You can make lots of money *and* help lots of people. The more money you make, the more people you can help—and with greater impact.

When a client says to me, "But I want to help as many people as possible!" I tell her, "Great. That's a noble goal, and you can absolutely do that. And here's exactly how you're going to do it. First, you're going to overhaul your business and pricing. You're going to increase your rates. You're going to start generating a healthy profit. You're going to create a surplus of cash—more than you personally need. And then you will take that surplus and use it to create an incredible program to help those in need."

Here's how a few clients took their surplus and used it to give back:

- One client granted a 100% scholarship for her post-mastectomy rehab program (a 12-month program) to one breast cancer survivor every year. So generous.

- Another began offering 10 "pay what you can" monthly memberships at her yoga studio. Life-changing.
- Another gifted one massage per month to a remarkable teacher nominated by community members. A beautiful way to give back.
- Another started running a weekly meditation class for veterans—free of charge. Imagine the ripple effect this creates.

Those are just a smattering of examples. There are hundreds more.

These business owners not only make money—and a lot of money, mind you—but they also make their services accessible to people in need. Greater impact. Less sacrifice. And the business owners I just mentioned are overjoyed to help people in need. They look forward to it. They are so grateful to be in a position where they can afford to do so! They show up to do their pro bono work well-rested, happy, and vibrant—not bedraggled and burdened with financial stress.

There's no doubt that receiving a scholarship can profoundly change the course of your life. I know because it happened to me.

When I was 26, after being laid off from my corporate sales job, I decided to pursue a Pilates certification so that I could one day open my own studio and run my own business. The Pilates teacher training program was $5,000, which, at the time, was an enormous amount of money for me. Newly married with our first mortgage payment—oh, and don't forget, I just lost my job, so we'd become a single-income household—my husband and I didn't know how we would swing the $5,000 tuition, plus all the supplementary classes and materials the program required. But I knew that opening a business would be our ticket to financial security, so I needed to find a way to enroll.

But the $5,000 tuition! Yikes! We didn't even have $5,000 in our savings account. So, I asked for help.

"I really want to enroll in this program, but I can't swing the $5,000 upfront cost," I embarrassedly typed in an email. "Is there an extended payment plan or a reduced tuition option for those who qualify?" I told her my story and promised that I would work hard in the program and be her star student.

Sure enough, the director of the program saw potential in me. She offered to give me a small price reduction plus a gradual payment plan over the course of six months. Thanks to this scholarship, I could enroll in the program and make it happen. Otherwise, the program would not have been an option for me.

Did the program director reduce the cost of tuition across the board to ensure that her program was accessible to everyone on earth? No! But when somebody came along with a lot of passion and potential, she was able to offer assistance.

There were 20 people enrolled in the Pilates program who paid the full $5,000 tuition upfront. This means the program director pocketed $100,000 (before minimal expenses). Flush with cash, she was in a position where she could offer assistance to someone like me, and it was no biggie. She was able to help me—because she was already profitable. When you're making great money, you can give back in powerful ways and create miracles for people who need help.

I want to drive this point home…

If you feel a spiritual calling to help those in need—people who are disenfranchised, oppressed, marginalized, or struggling financially—then go forth and serve those people, by all means. Serve. Assist. Change lives.

However, you need to pay yourself first before helping others. And, you need to find a way to serve those in need without putting yourself in financial distress.

Consider this question: How could you serve at the highest level without draining your bank account? Perhaps you could start a podcast to share your insights (free of charge) with a listenership of thousands or millions every week. Or write a weekly e-newsletter (also free) to provide life-changing tips for anyone who wants to read it. Or host a sliding scale workshop (once a month) open to the entire community. Once you're bringing home a hefty profit, you could use a portion of your profits to fund a scholarship program. There are innumerable ways you can do good—without depleting yourself.

You could do plenty of generous things—but first you need to shift your mindset. Instead of thinking, "I need to be accessible to everyone, which means lowering my prices," I want you to think, "I don't need to be accessible to everyone. I can increase my prices, generate a profit, and create financial security. Once I'm no longer in financial peril, I can give back in creative ways—without wrecking myself in the process."

I want you to say the following statements out loud to yourself:

I DO NOT NEED TO MAKE MYSELF ACCESSIBLE TO EVERYONE!

Say that again, one more time…

I DO NOT NEED TO MAKE MYSELF ACCESSIBLE TO EVERYONE!

I can make money and help people.

I deserve to make money while helping people.

Wanting to make money is not a bad thing.

The more money I make, the more people I can help.

I can't wait to have a surplus of cash to afford to start an incredible scholarship program, grant, award, or another initiative to give back on a higher level. I will get there. Soon.

Ultimately, it comes down to choices. What kind of life do you want to lead?

Do you want to offer free (or low-cost) services to 1,000 people—and end up shutting down your business because you can't afford to stay open? Or do you want to offer high-end premium services to 100 people, earn great money, keep your business running for decades, and then provide 10 full scholarships per year that powerfully impact 10 households in your community? Which path sounds more exciting? Which option would ultimately have a greater impact on humanity? Choose carefully. Price accordingly.

CHAPTER 7:

You Can Increase Your Prices Without Upsetting Your Clients

There are 7.753 billion people living on planet earth.

That is a vast number of people. And not everyone is going to like you.

You could be the most charming, gracious, kind, and generous person in the entire galaxy. You could be such a delight that you make Mr. Rogers look like an asshole in comparison! Nonetheless, there will be certain people (possibly millions of people) who just don't like you. Maybe they don't like your body, face, religion, political viewpoints, smell, the sound of your voice, the clothing you're wearing, the profession you've chosen, or your pricing.

You've got to find a way to be okay with not being liked. Whether it's therapy, coaching, or more wine, you have to accept that some people will admire you and others will not like you.

You're setting yourself up for a lifetime of misery if you don't.

It is not your responsibility to make everyone like you or convince everyone that your choices are the right ones. This includes your clients.

The only person who must like you and agree with you is you, because you are the only person who has to live with your decisions. Period.

Of course, we all want our clients to like us. That's natural. We want clients to agree with us. We want clients to cheer and celebrate for every decision we make! We want clients to toss roses and confetti in the air and say, "Hooray! You're increasing your prices!" and then release a flock of white doves while a brass marching band plays a merry tune! That would be the ideal scenario, of course! But this might not happen—and that is okay. Remember that your clients are not running your business. You are. When you undercut your pricing, you're the person who has to live with the consequences of that decision—not your clients.

Now, I imagine you've developed solid relationships with your clients. Some of your clients might even be close friends. In the past, you may have included them in your decision-making process, polling them to see what they want.

"Would you like for me to add a 5 a.m. class every morning?"

"How would you feel about us adding massage therapy to our menu of services?"

"If we created this new service package, would you be interested?"

And the absolute worst of all, "Would you be willing to pay this amount?"

You've probably spent years asking for validation and approval from your clients before making decisions. And you've probably shied away from certain decisions that are actually in the best interest of your business because you feared that your clients would disapprove.

Effective today, you will stop asking your clients for their approval and start running your business as if you own it, because you do. This means charging what you must charge, not what your clients would prefer you to charge.

"But, Erin, if I increase my prices, my clients won't like it. They'll complain. They'll send me angry emails. They'll make my life a living hell! Or worse, they'll say nothing—but quietly leave and take their business elsewhere," you protest.

"If you don't increase your prices," I counter, "you know what's going to happen next. You'll be broke. Your business won't survive. You'll have to close your doors. You'll become emotionally exhausted, sick, or worse."

"True," you concede. "But I don't know how to raise my prices without upsetting people."

Good news. I'll teach you. Later in this book—in Chapter 16—I explain how to roll out your new pricing successfully. I'll show you what to say—the exact wording to use—to get your clients excited about your new menu of premium offers and premium pricing. By doing a thoughtful rollout and communicating clearly, you can get the majority of your clients completely onboard—without causing a mass exodus of clients, protests, flaming pitchforks, or rioting in the streets. Yes, there will be a few grumblers, but they'll be the minority, not the majority.

Here's the thing: Nobody likes to pay more for services they already use, but guess what? Prices increase all the damn time, and we suck it up and pay the higher prices!

The cost of eggs once was $1.79, but today they cost $2.46. You still need the eggs to cook breakfast, right? Do you stamp your feet furiously in the grocery store, throw a tantrum, or send a scathing email to the shop owner? No! You plunk down your cash and pay whatever it costs.

A gallon of gas was once $2.99, but today it's $4.19—or in some areas of the country $6.99. You still need to fill up your tank, right? You shrug and go, "Well, it is what it is."

Do you want to pay more for these items? No! But do you? Yes! Because you understand that you need these items and that's just how much it costs.

The same is true for the services you sell to your clients. Most of your clients simply will not leave because you increase your prices. They might not like it at first, but they will understand that this is the new price they have to pay. They will suck it up and pay the higher prices so they can continue receiving your services.

"But my services are a luxury, not a necessity. My clients don't need my services," you might be thinking. To which I say, "Oh, but honey, they do!"

If you sell astrology readings, Reiki sessions, craniosacral massage, personal training, or another service that some deem non-essential, you might worry that raising your prices means goodbye to clients. Harken back to an earlier section of this book when I reminded you that you are not your client. Something that seems like a frivolous expense (to you, with your current budget) may be a must-have service (to your client).

Take me, for instance. I purchase certain services every month that many would consider luxuries but that I consider absolute necessities. The survival of my marriage, my children, and my personal well-being depends on these services. These are three non-negotiables in my household:

- Housekeeper
- Laundry delivery service
- Private chef (this sounds way more bougie than it actually is)

If each one of these service providers told me that the prices were increasing tomorrow—and several times they have—I would fork out the extra money every single time because I need these services! They're immensely valuable to me. They're important. I need them to function as a successful wife, mom, and business owner. Without these services, my family and I would be living in squalor, coated with a layer of filth, and eating Cheetos for dinner, and that's truly no exaggeration!

I need these service providers to be successful in keeping their businesses open. If paying more is what it takes, so be it!

If my housekeeper tells me he's closing his cleaning business because he's not making enough money, I would have to find another housekeeper. I don't want to find another housekeeper. Fabio has been cleaning my house—and cleaned my Pilates studio when I owned it—for over seven years. We've established a relationship. We've built trust. I don't want to start all over again with somebody I don't know. I want Fabio, so I'd rather pay more than find somebody else.

If my laundry delivery service closed because they filed for bankruptcy, I would have to do my own laundry, and, well, that's just not an option, my friend. I haven't done laundry since 2015, and I don't plan to pick it up again anytime soon. "How much is it going to cost me now?" "Okay, here's my card." No questions asked.

This goes for our lawn care service, gym memberships, daughters' gymnastics lessons, their musical theater camp, our wine of the month club, and so much more.

It's easier for your clients to pay you more than it is for them to find somebody new. It's that simple. Your clients want to see you succeed. They want you to stay in business. It's better for them that way! If it means they have to pay more, they will most of the time—because it's worth it to them!

Remember my client Martine? She's the one who second-guessed her decision to increase her prices—fearing that her clients would leave. But she eventually decided to trust the math and increase her prices anyway—setting her fears aside—and went from a -8% profit margin to a 21%.

Less than a month after increasing her prices, she posted this message inside my client support group:

"Hey, all. I just wanted to share what I've heard from one of my regular clients. I'm in the middle of switching over to memberships and substantial rate increases. This client wanted to clarify that the increase as it applies to her is 25%. She said, 'I totally understand if this is the business model that will keep your business prosperous. That is most important, and I respect that.' Another client who is getting a 30% increase—I emailed to verify that I was running her first charge with the new plan tomorrow—said, 'Absolutely. Thanks for checking in and all you do to keep this wonderful world going!' I mean, what???? I did not expect that!"

When you raise your prices, your best clients will support you wholeheartedly. The ones who don't, well, they weren't the clients you want anyway.

I think we're ready for some real talk now. What I'm about to say you won't like. It might even have you shaking in your boots a bit. But it needs to be said.

Once you increase your prices, not every client is going to stay—and this is completely okay.

Whenever you're experiencing an uplevel in your business, there will always be people who don't come along with you to that next level. This is a good thing. The clients who leave are making room for new clients who are your dream clients, your ideal clients, the kinds of clients who don't bat an eye at your prices because they know the value of what you provide and are happy to pay it.

This exact thing happened to my client Debbie. Remember Debbie—who went from begging for her hubby to be on our first call to being referred to as the "Profit Queen" by said husband? She raised her prices and then lost 20 members in one month. Ugh. That hurt! While the loss of those clients stung a little—okay, a lot—and while it temporarily had Debbie questioning her decision to work with me, she refused to let this be a setback. It was a step forward and upward.

Despite losing 20 clients, thanks to her new pricing model, she was actually making more money than she had in the past. So this wasn't a financial loss. It was a gain. Plus, those 20 people who left? They were her most challenging, unpleasant clients to begin with! Good riddance! Don't let the door hit you on the way out!

These clients didn't leave because Debbie increased her prices. In reality, they hadn't been happy for a long time, but they didn't feel as if they could leave. When Debbie increased her prices, they used this as an easy excuse to jump ship. In fact, the price increase made Debbie's life so much easier because it didn't require her to fire these clients herself—something she eventually would have had to do. Once they left, Debbie felt so much lighter. They were no longer draining her soul. They made room for new clients to come into the studio—fantastic people who Debbie and her staff absolutely love!

Losing a few clients due to a price increase can be a *good thing* because it leads to less stress, more money, and more space in your schedule to bring new clients on board—spaciousness to welcome new people who bring delight into your business—instead of a massive headache.

Have I convinced you that you can increase your prices without upsetting your clients? Or at least without upsetting your *ideal* clients? Hopefully yes. If not, I suspect that you fear, deep down, that you're simply not worthy of charging a higher price.

"What if I increase my prices but I'm not actually that good? What if clients pay the new prices and then feel like, 'That wasn't worth it?'"

Get cozy on the couch, my friend, because it's time for some therapy. Please note that I'm not qualified to conduct psychotherapy. But if I were qualified, you know what I would tell you?

I would tell you to "shut the fuck up!" My favorite mantra.

Whenever Negative Nelly rears her ugly head and tries to convince you that you are not worthy of the prices you need to charge, it is your duty to look her in the face and tell her to "shut the fuck up!"

Shut the fuck up! It's a highly effective method! I promise you!

If you are highly skilled at whatever service you provide, your clients love working with you, your clients sing your praises and keep coming back for additional appointments (or recommend you to their friends), then rest assured—you are GOOD at what you do. Not just good but excellent. Your services are valuable and appreciated. Your clients feel that paying you is completely "worth it." And most of your clients will continue to feel that way, even when your prices go up.

Repeat after me:

Not everyone will like me (or my pricing), and I am okay with that.

I don't have to convince everyone to agree with me.

I want my clients to be happy; however, I don't need their validation or approval on every decision I make. I need to do what's best for my company and for me.

I own my business. My clients do not.

My clients want me to succeed.

My clients understand that I need to generate a profit, which sometimes means increasing my prices.

My clients know the value of the services I provide, and they are happy to pay more.

My dream clients won't leave simply because I raise my prices. They will stay.

My nightmare clients will grumble and then leave when I raise my prices. Thank God. Good riddance. Bye.

When I increase my prices, I create space for dream clients to pour in.

I titled this chapter "You can increase your prices without upsetting your clients." While that's true, an even more accurate statement would be: "You can increase your prices without upsetting your *best* clients." Or at least, without upsetting the majority of your clients. Because the fact is, you're probably going to upset a handful of people—and that is okay. It doesn't mean it's the wrong move. It's still the right choice.

There are moments in life when you need to do the right thing—the hard thing, the scary thing—even if it means certain people aren't going to like it. You have to be courageous and do it anyway. Your courage will be rewarded—with higher profits, a more spacious schedule, more ideal clients, and fewer headache-inducing clients.

Even if you lose a few people along the way, ultimately, you win.

CHAPTER 8:
You Are Making a Choice Every Time You Undercharge

If you made it this far in the book, you know it's time to overhaul your prices.

You know it's going to be challenging. You know it will test your strength and rattle your confidence. You know there will be moments when your inner Negative Nelly screams at you, "You can't do this, you idiot!" and you have to scream back, "Shut the fuck up!"

But more importantly, you know that this is what you *must do* to start living the life you truly desire. No more settling. No more accepting that this current reality is the only life possible for you. You are ready to take a stand. You are ready to overhaul your business, your pricing, and your life.

Just in case you're still waffling a bit, wondering, "Do I *really* need to overhaul my pricing? Is this necessary? Couldn't I just skip this?"... I want to leave you with one more thought.

Look at your business today. Take a good hard look. Don't try to sugarcoat it and make yourself feel better about its current state of affairs. Ask yourself honestly, "Is my business the business of my dreams? Is my business providing me with the life I truly want?" If you answered, "No," then it's time to make a change. And the first thing you must change is your pricing.

Jim Rohn, entrepreneur and motivational speaker, says it best:

"Your life does not get better by chance. It gets better by change."

Change is not easy. Change is not always fun. Change can be one of the scariest things you undertake. But change is necessary if you want a different outcome.

Of course, it's your business. It's your life. So it's your choice. Nobody can make the choice for you. #prochoice

You can continue undercutting your prices and operating your business as you've done in the past. But if you do this, understand that you are making a *choice*, and choices have consequences.

If you undercharge, this means you're choosing to work an additional 10, 20, or 30 hours per week to generate the income you need to survive.

If you undercharge, this means you're choosing to work 50 weeks a year with only two weeks of vacation (if you're lucky) as if you're an employee in a dead-end job.

If you undercharge, this means you're choosing to experience high levels of stress and worry on a daily basis, poor sleep, and frazzled nerves, sacrificing your health and well-being. (Cortisol has a nasty effect on our bodies.)

If you undercharge, this means you're choosing to pay yourself less and live paycheck-to-paycheck—only one disaster away from losing everything.

Like I said. Choices have consequences.

How do these consequences look in real life? It can look like having to work on holidays and never taking a real break. It might be missing a girlfriend's wedding because you are too broke, stressed, tired, or busy to make the trip. It might be skipping school pick-up with your kids because you need to squeeze in "one more email" or "one more client," and you can't afford to step away from your desk.

Suppose you're cool with that, cool. If you're not cool with that, then you need to make a different choice.

By making one choice in your business—the choice to overhaul your prices—you're choosing a different life for yourself. A new and better life that looks like this:

- Working only 42 weeks a year
- Taking ten weeks off every year (paid time off)
- Working less than 30 hours per week
- Going on vacation—correction—multiple vacations each year
- Spending holidays with your family and friends
- Actively participating in your children's lives
- Breathing easily because you know you've got plenty of cash in the bank to cover whatever arises next—whether it's an unexpected bill, crisis, or something positive—like an exciting investment opportunity.

Isn't that the kind of life you'd choose if given the choice?

I know how scary it is to overhaul your prices. Remember, I was there. Sitting in that hospital room, fighting meningitis, evaluating my business and life, and realizing, "Things cannot continue this way. My brain is literally swelling with pain, inflamed with infection. And it's all because I am overworking and undercharging. I chose this. And I have the power to choose something new." I knew what I needed to do. Nonetheless, I was terrified to do it.

Ultimately, my desire to provide a better life for myself and my family won— because this desire was much stronger than my fears. I wanted so much more for myself and my family. I *deserved* so much more. We—myself, my husband, and kids—we all deserved more. My kids deserved a mom who wasn't working 50 to 60 hours a week, exhausted, and placed on mandatory bed rest. I'm asking you, reader: What is the desire inside of you that is bigger, stronger, and mightier than your fears?

After that hospital visit all those years ago, I made a choice. And that choice changed the trajectory of my life.
Today, I work an average of 20 hours per month. I take off roughly 16 weeks each year. I travel 6-12 times per year (just this year, I've traveled to France twice—once by myself for nine days—Belgium, Tanzania with my family for

safari, LA, Oregon, and the Blue Ridge Mountains). I pay myself multiple six figures. That's my *salary.* Not my business revenue prior to subtracting expenses or taxes. Salary. As in take-home pay that goes directly into my personal bank account.

On the daily, I pick my daughters up from school and take them to their activities—and I treasure these sweet moments riding around together in the minivan. I work out every morning. I take an hour-long bath every evening (true story: I wrote most of this book while lounging in the tub surrounded by scented bubbles!). I enjoy nightly family dinners. I connect with my girlfriends. I sip wine with my husband in our tropical backyard oasis by the pool. I binge-watch Netflix and bad reality TV—I'm a *Bachelor* addict and I'm not ashamed to admit it!

I live my fucking life! And I *love* my fucking life.

I'm not sharing these details to boast or irritate you. ("Oh, how nice for you, Erin, so glad you're living your Best Bubble Life!" *snarky eye roll*) I'm sharing this to demonstrate what is possible. I have created my dream life. I want (more than anything) for you to have your dream life too. This is doable. This is what happens when you make the courageous choice to overhaul your pricing.

Many people love to pretend "money doesn't matter," but the reality is that it does matter. Money matters. Time matters. Health matters. All precious resources matter.

So, my friend, it's time. Time for you to make the choice to change. Change your business. Change your life.

And that is exactly what you will do in *Part Two: Overhaul Your Pricing.*

In Part Two, I teach you exactly how to overhaul your pricing step by step. You're going to plug numbers into a spreadsheet. You're going to calculate profit margins. You're going to do some serious adulting, and I promise it will be simpler than you think. Can you type a few numbers into a screen and then press "enter?" Of course you can. You're no fool! You're not a nincompoop!

So, you can absolutely do everything I'm about to teach you.

Before moving into the next section, it's important to remember that the numbers do not lie.

2 + 2 always equals 4. You cannot argue with math.

The same goes for your business numbers. When you do the math and the math gives you a very specific number, don't question it. Sure, feel free to "check your work" if you want to double-check that you entered the numbers correctly, but don't question the math. When you come up with the exact same number for the second, third, or fourth time, trust it.

Do you know why you can trust the math? Because math is what it is. It's unemotional. While *you* may have great, tough, emotional, and moody days, math is stable and constant. It never changes. Once you understand this, you can rely on math to lead you to success. You might not trust yourself (at least right now), but you can trust the math.

Part One: Summary

Now that you've reached the end of *Part One: Shift Your Mindset,* let's do a quick recap.

More than anything else, this is what I want you to know:

- If you want to stay in business and take care of yourself and your family, then you need to overhaul your pricing. You need to create a new pricing model that allows you to work less and make more.

- This is non-negotiable. This is a must-do step in running your business. You must do it just like feeding your kids or paying your electricity bill. Either do this or close your doors.

- You have to do this. Period.

- When you overhaul your prices, the impact is immediate and very exciting. This will get you where you want to be in your business and life.

- If you are unsatisfied with your business, you need to make new choices to get to where you want to be.

- Your current situation is hard. Changing your situation is hard. Choose your hard. Do you want to choose the hard that keeps you where you are? Or the hard that leads to somewhere better?

- In one year, you can be exactly where you are now—or in an even worse place. Or you can be somewhere different. Somewhere better. This year is going to fly by either way. Where do you want to be?

- Shifting your mindset is the first step of the process. However, if you are struggling to shift your mindset, I suggest focusing less on your mindset and simply looking at the math. You cannot argue with the math. What does the spreadsheet tell you? It is unemotional. It doesn't have hang-ups and blocks.

- Sometimes, you need to give yourself tough love. Tell yourself, "Self, I hear you. I get that you're anxious. I get that you have a lot of feelings about this and you're uncomfortable making a change, but with all due respect, shut the fuck up. I need to look at the numbers and not get derailed by emotion. This is an important change I need to make."

P.S. If all else fails, more wine.

P.P.S. I'll see you in *Part Two: Overhaul Your Pricing*. This is the best part. This is my jam. I'm so pumped to walk you through the process and awaken your inner Badass Math Ninja.

Head to Part Two and I'll meet you there.

If I want to become the best provider in my field (the best yoga teacher, the best massage therapist, the best attorney, etc.) what would that look like? How could I provide an even better experience for each client and truly blow them away?

_____

_____

_____

_____

_____

Do I want to be the discount provider of my industry? The bargain cheapo option? Or do I want to be the best—the premium provider with premium pricing?

_____

_____

_____

_____

_____

_____

If I was hiring someone else to do my job, what would that person's base salary be? Currently, am I paying myself (at least) that much?

_____

_____

_____

_____

_____

_____

If I continue to undercharge, what are the consequences of this choice? Immediate consequences? Long-term consequences?

_____

_____

_____

_____

_____

_____

If I raise my prices to an appropriate level—so that I can pay myself a healthy salary and generate a profit on top of that—how would this change my life?

_____

_____

_____

_____

_____

_____

_____

What are the areas of my business (or life) where I have been handing over my power to somebody else? (To my husband, dad, accountant, or anyone else?)

_____

_____

_____

_____

_____

_____

_____

What would happen if I started believing, "I am good with numbers." If I believe that, what kind of ripple effect would happen in my business and life?

_____

_____

_____

_____

_____

_____

PART TWO

Overhaul Your Pricing

Before You Dive in...

Before embarking on this next section, I'd like to offer a suggestion. From years of experience working with hundreds of clients, I have found that the best approach is to take it "one step at a time"—literally. Work through the math one number, one line, and one calculation at a time.

The formula for calculating your ideal pricing is layered. One equation builds upon the next, so it's imperative that each calculation is accurate before moving on to the next.

For this reason, I recommend reading Chapter 9 completely—maybe even two or three times, if needed—and then stop, take your time, and do the math before moving on to Chapters 10, 11, 12, and beyond. Do this for each chapter in *Part Two: Overhaul Your Pricing*. It will make the process much easier for you!

You'll see a worksheet (or two) at the end of each chapter.

You can fill out these worksheets manually—grab a pencil, write your business numbers into the worksheet, then press a few buttons on your calculator to find the results. Super easy.

Or fill out these worksheets online. To do that, scan the QR code (it looks like a square barcode) with your phone, tablet, or any device. This QR code will bring you to a webpage where you can fill out the worksheet online. Voila! Type in your numbers on the screen, click "Enter," and boom. The math gets done for you.

Whether you prefer to write directly in this book or work online, please do whatever is simplest for you. My goal is to make this as easy for you as possible!

Most of all, remember: *You are good at math.* If any voices arise in your head and try to convince you otherwise, firmly tell those unwanted voices to shut the fuck up.

Happy calculating!

CHAPTER 9:
Do a Profit Analysis

In order to improve any part of your life—whether it's your messy closet stuffed with way-too-small jeans from 2003, your marriage, or your finances—the first step is to assess the current situation and accept where you are.

You need to take an honest look at what's going on.

You have to know where you're starting to figure out where you're going.

This is absolutely true when beginning your Pricing Overhaul®. You must know the current state of your business before you can make positive changes. But how do you uncover the reality of your current situation? You start by conducting a *profit analysis*.

WHAT IS A PROFIT ANALYSIS?

When you do a profit analysis, you look at how much money is coming in, how much money is going out, where the money is going, and how much money is left over (aka your profit)—when it's all said and done.

That's it. It's actually very simple.

However, most business owners have never conducted a profit analysis. Why? You might think, "That sounds like something only 'big companies' need to do, not a small business like mine." Wrong. Every business needs to do this.

Or you may think, "Well, surely this is something my accountant ought to do. It's their job. Not mine." Also wrong. (No more giving your financial power away to other people!)

Or you reckon, "Hmm, a profit analysis? This sounds really complex. It's probably too advanced for my tiny womanly pea-brain to handle!" Ugh. The wrongest!

Doing a profit analysis is simpler than you think, and it's absolutely crucial to do it.

ARE "PROFIT" AND "REVENUE" THE SAME THING?

No, they are not. *Revenue* is how much money you bring in the door. *Profit* is how much is left over after you've paid various expenses (yes, including paying yourself).

In layman's terms, *gross revenue* is the total amount of cash your business generated over the course of the year. In other words, all the money you generated through your business. Every service you sold, every invoice that got paid, every dime you earned.

It's easy for business owners to get glamoured by revenue. You see your sales increasing month-over-month, year-over-year, and you think to yourself—naively—"Look how much money I'm making! My business is killing it." Hate to break it to you, sista, but your business is not killing it (although it might be killing you) unless it's profitable. Without a profit, your business is only one or two bad months away from *being* killed.

You could be generating ten million dollars per year in gross revenue. Your business could be in a dire, precarious situation because your ten-million-dollar business might have a 0% profit margin. Ten million coming in. Ten million going out. Nothing left at the end of the year, zero, not one penny. See what I mean? Gross revenue is important, but it's not the *only* number that matters.

Revenue is *not* the key indicator of a prosperous business. Your profit margin *is*—that's the percentage of cash that your business gets to keep.

The more your business keeps, the healthier it is, and the longer it will remain open. And the more likely it is to survive a catastrophe—like a global pandemic, hurricane, flood, fire, cyber attack, data breach, PR scandal, personal family matter that pulls you away from work for an extended period of time, or any other challenge that might arise.

HOW DO YOU CALCULATE A PROFIT MARGIN?

Here's an example. If your business generates $100 in revenue and keeps $10 after all expenses are paid, then your profit margin is 10%.

How did I get that number?

I took the $10 kept and divided it by the $100 generated.

10 / 100 = 0.1

Then, to turn that decimal into a percentage, I multiplied it by 100.

0.1 x 100 = 10%

It's that easy!

While that math was nice and easy, a 10% profit margin is not so nice.

WHAT IS THE IDEAL PROFIT MARGIN?

Ideally, for a service-based business, you want to have a minimum 30% profit margin. Emphasis on *minimum* because the sky's the limit when it comes to profit. The higher, the better! There are certain things, like profit margins and Dolly Parton's hair, that should always be as high as possible! But a solid benchmark for service-based businesses is 30%. (Vogue Beauty, 2017)

When you conduct your first profit analysis—which I'm about to show you how to do—you might find that your profit margin is dismal. I'm talking about no profit at all, or worse, a negative profit margin—yes, it is possible to have a negative profit margin—which means that your business is actually losing money each month. Yikes.

If you find yourself faced with an abysmal profit margin or you discover that you're actually losing money, well, that explains why you're in debt and never have cash on hand. This fucking sucks. And this is temporary. Don't sweat it because once you overhaul your pricing, your profit margin will start to climb!

Before you calculate your profit margin, there are two other margins we need to discuss:

- Operating expense margin
- Payroll expense margin

Let me break this down for you.

WHAT IS AN OPERATING EXPENSE MARGIN?

Your *operating expense margin* includes all expenses necessary to run your business.

This includes fixed monthly expenses—expenses you can expect to pay month after month without fail. Such as:

- Rent or mortgage (if you own a brick-and-mortar business)
- Utilities (electricity, water, etc.)
- Insurance
- Phone
- Internet
- Any other expenses that keep your business doors open. Think, "If I missed this payment one month, I'd be in trouble."

Your operating expense margin also includes one-time, non-recurring expenses. Expenses that happen once a year or sporadically throughout the year but not every month. Such as:

- Annual renewal fee to keep your license valid
- Maintenance work on your A/C when it went out in the dead of summer
- Business taxes for sales, use, service, and property
- Basically, every single expense that your business paid during the year

Add it all together—fixed monthly expenses + one-time, non-recurring expenses—and that's how you figure out your total operating expenses.

Ideally, your operating expense margin should be no more than 35% of your gross revenue.

Using the same example above, if you generate $100 in revenue but you spend $50 of that to pay your operating expenses, well then, your operating expense margin is 50%. That's too much! Remember, you're aiming for 35%. It's time to look at how much money is going out—and where it's going—so that you can either dial back your operating expenses or increase your revenue to compensate (or possibly both).

WHAT IS A PAYROLL EXPENSE MARGIN?

To figure out your *payroll expense margin*, add up all of your payroll expenses for all staff members—employees and independent contractors—including:

- Gross wages (total compensation paid by the business before employment taxes withholding)
- Employer-matched payroll taxes for social security and medicare
- 401K contributions paid by the business
- Employer-sponsored health insurance
- Paid time off
- Your owner's salary. That's assuming you are an owner-operator.

"What's an owner operator?" you wonder.

"Thanks for asking. I'm so glad you did!" *wink wink*

An *owner-operator* is an owner who works inside her business. Meaning that if the owner decided to stop working altogether, she would have to pay somebody else to do her job in her place. Otherwise, the business would come to a screeching halt and stop generating revenue altogether.

If you're reading this book, I'm 99% sure this describes you as an owner. So the amount you would have to pay somebody else to do your job is the amount you should be paying yourself—mind-blowing concept, huh? And you must include that amount in your payroll expense margin.

Back to calculating your payroll expense margin…once you've totaled all of your payroll expenses, you then need to divide it by your total gross revenue.

For consistency, using that same $100 revenue generated, let's pretend you spend $40 on payroll. That would mean that your payroll expense margin is 40%.

Like your operating expense margin, you want your payroll expense margin to be at or below 35%.

COMPARE THREE SCENARIOS

Take a look at the following three imaginary scenarios.

You can see how, by adjusting certain numbers, you can shift a business from "pretty terrible" to "much better" and eventually "excellent."

Business with a 10% profit margin (pretty terrible)
    Gross revenue: $100
    Operating expenses: $50 (margin: 50%)
    Payroll expenses: $40 (margin: 40%)
    Profit: $10 (margin: 10%)

Business with a 30% profit margin (much better)
  Gross revenue: $100
  Operating expenses: $35 (margin: 35%)
  Payroll expenses: $35 (margin: 35%)
  Profit: $30 (margin: 30%)

Business with a 50% profit margin (excellent!)
  Gross revenue: $100
  Operating expenses: $25 (margin: 25%)
  Payroll expenses: $25 (margin: 25%)
  Profit: $50 (margin: 50%)

I just threw a lot of numbers at you. Now's a good time to repeat to yourself, "I am good at math. I am good at math. I am good at math." Really, you are.

Ultimately, it all boils down to this: You want your business to have more money coming in than going out. You don't need to have a Ph.D. in advanced calculus and linear algebra to understand why this is important.

Like I said earlier, I urge my clients to create a 30% profit margin, minimum.

Here's an easy way to remember this.

---

35 / 35 / 30

35% goes to operating expenses
35% goes to payroll expenses (including paying yourself)
30% is profit!

35 / 35 / 30

Embroider that onto a decorative throw pillow and stare at it daily!

It should go without saying, the lower your operating and payroll expense margins are, the higher your profit margin will be!

As I said before, the sky's the limit when it comes to profit. One of the most exhilarating things about being self-employed is the fact that you have the potential to generate unlimited profit. You can build a business that produces $100K in profit each year, $500K, or $10 million, and beyond. You're limited only by your imagination and ambition.

Picture a business with 30 / 30 / 40 margins. Or 25 / 25 / 50 margins. Shoot, I've worked with online businesses that have 10 / 10 / 80 margins (since they're virtual businesses with no physical office location, no physical product inventory, and very minimal operating expenses, they can achieve massive profit margins, which is quite a delight!) Cue the band: "We're in the money. We've got a lot of what it takes to get along."

brief pause as we picture Ginger Rogers high-kicking across the stage as dollar bills rain down!

You may wonder, "What are my operating expense margins, payroll expense margins, and profit margins right now? I honestly have no idea."

Well, sugarplum, we're about to find out because it's time for you to do... drumroll...your first profit analysis.

HOW TO DO A PROFIT ANALYSIS: STEP BY STEP

Here is your assignment:

I want you to conduct a profit analysis on your business.

If it's January or February—and the previous year ended fairly recently—you can do a profit analysis for last year.

Or if it's March, April, May, or later, I recommend that you do a profit analysis for this year-to-date (YTD). That's January 1st through today!

Date range being analyzed:

_____

Here's exactly how you do this. Follow along, step by step.

Step 1: Find out your gross revenue.

How much money did you bring in the door during the date range being analyzed?

Add up all your sales—every single dollar your business has generated by selling products, services, programs, workshops, seminars, packages, or whatever you sell. Total it up to find your gross revenue.

If you're thinking, "I have no fucking idea how much I've generated! It's all such a mess! Lord only knows!" (*collapse onto the floor, sobbing, dry-heaving*) Well, now is the moment to find out! Cleanup on aisle five! Let's address this mess.

Take a look at your bank account, PayPal account, Square, Stripe, Wave, Venmo, or whatever system(s) you use to take payments from clients. Log in. Run a report to find out your earnings for a specific date range, such as January 1st to today. If you are not sure how to do this, check the FAQs or contact customer service and ask for help. Do whatever you need to do to get the information you need. This is a put-on-your-big-girl-panties moment. You need to do this.

If you use multiple payment methods (some clients pay you in cash, some pay via check, some pay on Venmo, etc.), you need to total it up to find your gross revenue.

You can (and must) do this. Take the time you need to do this right before moving on to the next step. If that means clearing your schedule for one whole day to dig in and find the numbers, do that.

Once you've figured out your gross revenue for the date range being analyzed, move on to Step 2.

What's your total gross revenue?

_____

Step 2: Find out your operating expenses.

How much money have you sent *out* the door during the date range being analyzed?

Add up all of your fixed monthly expenses + one-time, non-recurring expenses. All expenses (*except* for paying people—employees, contractors, and yourself. We'll do that separately). Total it up to find your operating expenses.

Same recommendation as above. Take your time with this. You might need to block out an entire day to gather all of your receipts, go through your bank statements, and figure this out. That's okay. Take plenty of time so that you don't feel rushed and frazzled. Once that's done, move to step 3.

How much did you spend on operating expenses?

_____

Step 3: Find out your payroll expenses.

How much money did you pay to employees, contractors, and yourself during the date range being analyzed? How much did you pay in payroll taxes and employee benefits?

Add it all up to find your payroll expenses.

How much did you spend on payroll expenses?

_____

Step 4: Find out your net profit.

Plug the following numbers into your calculator:

Gross revenue (minus) operating expenses (minus) payroll expenses. What's left is your net profit.

For instance, $100 (minus) $50 (minus) $40 means $10 is left.

Gross revenue _____

−

Operating expenses _____

−

Payroll expenses _____

= _____

Step 5: Find out your operating expense margin.

Type into your calculator your operating expense (divided by) gross revenue. Press enter. Then multiply that number by 100 to get your operating expense margin—as a percentage.

For instance, $50 (divided by) $100 is 0.50. Multiply this by 100, and you get 50%. That means the operating expense margin is what now? Say it with me: 50%. That's right.

Operating expenses   _____

/

Gross revenue   _____

Your answer   _____ * 100

=   _____ %

Step 6: Find out your payroll expense margin.

Exactly the same thing we just did.

Type into your calculator your payroll expense (divided by) gross revenue. Press enter. Then multiply that number by 100 to get your payroll expense margin—as a percentage.

For instance, $40 (divided by) $100 is 0.40. Multiply this by 100, and you get 40%. That means the payroll expense margin is 40%.

Payroll expense   _____

/

Gross revenue   _____

```
Your answer    _____ * 100

=              _____ %
```

Pause to reward yourself with a cool glass of iced tea, lemonade, or frosty rosé. Look at you. Doing math. This is next-level adulting! You're doing fantastic so far.

Step 7: Find out your profit margin.

Type your net profit (which you calculated in Step 4) into a calculator and (divide by) your gross revenue. Press enter. Then multiply that number by 100 to get your profit margin—as a percentage.

Example: $10 (divided by) $100 is 0.10. Multiply that by 100, and you get 10%.

```
Net profit     _____
/
Gross revenue  _____

Your answer    _____ * 100

=              _____ %
```

Step 8: Take a look at your three margins, side by side

What is your operating expense margin, payroll expense margin, and profit margin? You just calculated all of these.

Write 'em down.

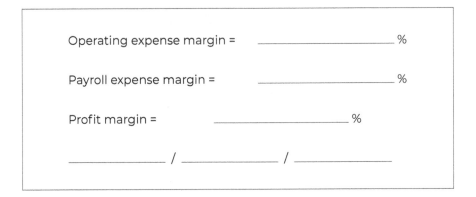

Operating expense margin = _____ %

Payroll expense margin = _____ %

Profit margin = _____ %

_____ / _____ / _____

Right now, your margins might be 50 / 40 / 10…or…50 / 30 / 20…or…70 / 15 / 15…or something else entirely.

Compare those margins to the 35 / 35 / 30 benchmark—which is the gold standard for a healthy service-based business.

Are you pretty close to that ideal benchmark? Or way off? Perhaps you're so far off that you're practically in another solar system?

Whatever the case may be, do not judge yourself. These are just numbers. These numbers say nothing about your intelligence, abilities, potential, or what your future is going to look like. I said it before. I will say it again. These numbers spell out where you are starting. Not where you're going.

YOUR PROFIT ANALYSIS IS COMPLETE

How'd you do?! Not exactly where you hoped you would be? It's okay. What's important is that now you have a clear picture of what's actually going on with your business. You know the numbers. This is a huge step. You might not like what you're seeing, but you can confront it, accept it, and choose to do something to improve it.

If you currently have a negative profit margin, 0% profit margin, or a very tiny profit margin like 5% or 10%, that's not exactly thrilling, but it's all about to change. We're going to get you to a 30% profit margin—the absolute bare minimum—and upward from there!

QUICK SUMMARY

Let's review a few terms we discussed in this chapter.

Gross revenue - Your total sales for the year (or year-to-date). All the money you've brought in the door.

Operating expenses - Add up your fixed monthly expenses and one-time, non-recurring expenses for the year (or year-to-date). The grand total is your operating expenses. (Note: Add up all expenses you've paid, except for paying employees, contractors, or yourself. That's separate.)

Payroll expenses - Add up everything you paid employees, contractors, and yourself for the year (or year-to-date), including wages, plus all the extras like payroll taxes, medicare, social security, Federal Unemployment Tax Act (FUTA), bonuses, and all the bells and whistles. The grand total is your payroll expenses.

Net profit - Take your gross revenue, subtract operating expenses, subtract payroll expenses, and what is left? That's your net profit. It might be nonexistent or small right now. That's going to change.

Margins - Compared to your gross revenue, what percentage is your net profit? That's your profit margin. What percentage are your operating expenses? That's your operating expense margin. And so on. A margin is simply a percentage of your gross revenue.

Profit analysis - That's when you review all the numbers—gross revenue, operating expenses, payroll expenses, and net profit—to find out your margins.

Ideal margins - Ideally, if you're running a service-based business, you want your operating expense margin, payroll margin, and profit margin to be 35 / 35 / 30, which means 35%, 35%, and 30% of your gross revenue.

Eventually, I want to see your profit margin higher than 30%. We'll discuss how to achieve that later in this book.

Badass Math Ninja - That's you. See also: courageous entrepreneur, business owner on-the-rise, serious grown-up, woman with unlimited potential.

CHAPTER 10:

Get Control Of Your Operating Expenses

You just completed your first profit analysis. Or perhaps the first one you've done in a very long time. Congratulations! You did it! Even if the margins aren't where you'd love them to be, doesn't *knowing* feel so good?

If you are the rare soul who actually discovered that your margins are miraculously in healthy ranges, congratu-fucking-lations because that is no small feat!

But if I had to guess, most likely, you discovered that your operating expense margin is way higher than 35%. It's okay. Most are upon first calculations. But in this chapter, you're going to get all of your operating expenses organized and in check—so that you can increase your profit margin and start living your dream life.

Let's assume your operating expense margin is currently higher than 35%. You might be freaking out, thinking, "How in the world am I spending that much money?" This, my friend, is what we'll get a handle on right now.

EXPENSES ARE NOT BAD

Here's the first thing I want to emphasize: Expenses are not bad! I repeat! Expenses are not bad!

It costs money to make money. Your business is going to have expenses, and most of those expenses are necessary to continue running your business.

PROFIT-GENERATING EXPENSES

Some expenses are *profit-generating expenses*. For example, marketing expenses, which yield a high return on investment. This might include printing flyers and putting them around town, paying a monthly fee for your e-newsletter software so that you can keep in contact with your clientele, or purchasing social media ads.

Perhaps you know (for a fact) that these expenses bring you new clients every single month, which means that without these expenses, you'd be making less.

INVESTMENT EXPENSES

You might also have *investment expenses*. Such as hiring a coach, consultant, or trainer; enrolling in a course; or doing continuing education to maintain a competitive edge in your field. These expenses might not immediately lead to cash in the bank—but they're important because they support your overall development as a business owner.

WHICH TO KEEP AND WHICH TO CUT?

As you're taking a closer look at your operating expenses, resist the urge to go on a cutting spree—eliminating every expense. Sure, you may discover that some expenses are unnecessary—like that monthly $14.99 subscription for an online service you completely forgot you even had—and it's okay to let those go. Please do.

But it's important to remember that you don't need to eliminate every single expense. If you trim things too leanly, you're setting yourself up for failure, not success.

"But how do I decide which expenses to keep and which ones to reduce or eliminate?" you may wonder.

Here's what I recommend.

Ask yourself, "If I eliminate this expense, will my job and life be easier or more difficult?" If you answered, "More difficult," then that's a justifiable expense that should be kept.

Here are a few examples:

- Bookkeeper: "My job would definitely be more difficult without her." = Keep

- Janitorial service: "Yeah. I don't have time to clean the toilets and scrub the floors. My job would definitely be more difficult without this." = Keep

- Adobe Photoshop subscription: "I totally forgot I was even paying for this. I had every intention of learning Photoshop, but I never did. My job would be easier without this hanging over my head." = Eliminate

- Part-time assistant: "I love my assistant and want to keep her on the payroll. However, I'm realizing I need to update her weekly list of duties. There are certain things she does that really aren't important anymore. There are better things she could be doing with her time." = Keep but make some adjustments

YOUR BUSINESS EXPENSES ARE WHATEVER *YOU* DECIDE THEY NEED TO BE

You're the business owner. Only *you* get to decide what's a crucial business expense and what's not.

For example, one crucial expense (for my business) is "travel to attend retreats and events." I give myself an annual allowance for these types of expenses because I know that retreats and events are necessary to my development as a business owner and provide me with opportunities to network and meet new clients. This is a must-do for me.

So, I include this in my operating expenses. By automatically including "travel to attend retreats and events" in my operating expenses, this means that I never have to say "no" to these types of opportunities when they arise because I always have the cash to pay for them.

I tell my clients, "Once you've decided what your operating expenses are going to be, you need to bake these expenses into your pricing." You're going to price your services so that your expenses are automatically covered, and you don't have to worry about it. That way, you're planning ahead smartly—instead of being shocked, stunned, gobsmacked, and emotionally derailed when an expense arises.

FIXED MONTHLY VS. ONE-TIME, NON-RECURRING

There are two types of operating expenses you want to identify:

- Fixed monthly expenses
- One-time, non-recurring expenses

As I mentioned in the previous chapter, your *fixed monthly expenses* are the expenses you can expect to pay every single month on repeat. These are expenses your business cannot live without.

I'm talking about the electricity in your spa—you can't inject Botox in the dark, or I suppose you could but please don't! The Internet—you can't Zoom with your clients if your WiFi is down. The rent—you can't teach group Pilates classes if you're facing eviction. Coffee beans for your clinic's kitchen area—perhaps you will shrivel up and become comatose without them!

Other fixed monthly expenses may include your advertising, business loan repayments, dues and subscriptions, cleaning and laundry service, etc. Toward the end of this chapter, I put a loooo-ooooong list of fixed monthly expenses—just about every expense imaginable.

The next operating expense category is *one-time, non-recurring expenses*. Think large payments that happen one time per year or periodically every once in a while. Examples include your annual professional liability insurance premium, your year-end payment to your accountant for your business tax preparation, that new piece of furniture you purchased for your waiting room, or the continuing education workshop you took.

Do you want to rebrand your business? That's a one-time, non-recurring expense. The computer crashed, and you need to replace it? That's a one-time, non-recurring expense. Or, if you're like me, there's a business retreat taking place in Bali and you want to attend? That's a one-time, non-recurring expense. Although these expenses don't recur each month—and some might never occur again—you still want to bake the amounts into your pricing so that when one-time, non-recurring expenses arise in the future, you always have the cash to pay for them.

That's exactly what you're going to do now. You will *itemize*—that's a fancy way of saying make a list of—all of your fixed monthly expenses and your one-time, non-recurring expenses. Then, add them all together to calculate your *total monthly operating expenses*.

HOW TO CALCULATE YOUR TOTAL MONTHLY OPERATING EXPENSES: STEP BY STEP

Step 1: Find out your fixed monthly expenses.

Take a look at the worksheet below.

Fill it out to make a list of all the fixed monthly expenses you currently pay. Next to each item, write the monthly amount you pay.

Forgetting something? Go online and download your last three months' bank statements and/or credit card statements. Review those. Double-check and see, "Are there any fixed monthly expenses I might be forgetting?" If so, add them to your list.

Add it up to find out, "Here's how much I pay in fixed monthly expenses every month."

Fixed Operating Expenses

Category	Monthly Payment	Date Paid
ADVERTISING Google ads, Facebook ads, direct mail, radio, magazine ads, coupon booklets, etc.		
DEBT Economic Injury Disaster Loan (EIDL), business loan, credit cards, etc.		
DUES AND SUBSCRIPTIONS Spotify, Amazon Prime, QuickBooks Online, trade organizations, etc.		
EQUIPMENT Audio-visual equipment, LED lighting equipment, etc.		

Category	Monthly Payment	Date Paid
INSURANCE General liability insurance, commercial property insurance, etc.		
MERCHANT FEES Fees taken by Venmo, Stripe, PayPal, etc.		
PHONE/INTERNET Mobile phone, landline, high-speed Internet, etc.		
PROFESSIONAL FEES Accountant, bookkeeper, attorney, consultant, biz coach, etc.		
EDUCATION Workshops, classes, seminars, expenses for continuing education units (CEUs), etc.		

Category	Monthly Payment	Date Paid
RENT Brick and mortar business location rent, office rent, etc.		
REPAIRS/MAINTENANCE Cleaning service, laundry service, window cleaning, HVAC service plan, etc.		
SECURITY Security cameras, alarm system, motion sensors, etc.		
WEBSITE/HOSTING GoDaddy, Lunapages, web developer, etc.		

Category	Monthly Payment	Date Paid
SOFTWARE/SCHEDULING Mindbody Online, Wellness Living, Acuity, etc.		
SUPPLIES/PURCHASES Towels, toilet paper, paper, pens, etc.		
UTILITIES Water, heating/cooling, electricity, gas, trash/recycling, etc.		
OTHER		
TOTAL EXPENSES	$	

Step 2: Find out your one-time, non-recurring expenses.

Same thing, once again. Make a list of all the one-time, non-recurring expenses you paid in one year. Next to each one, write the amount you paid.

Just like before, this is a good moment to review your bank statements and/or credit card statements from the last year. Go through carefully and hunt for any expenses you forgot about. "Oh right, I pay that annual membership fee for such-and-such." That sort of thing.

Add it up to find out, "Here's how much I pay in one-time, non-recurring expenses over the course of one year."

Divide that number by 12 to find out, "Here's the average amount per month."

One-time, Non-recurring Expenses		
Name	Annual Payment	Date Paid
TOTAL EXPENSES	$	

Total spent = _____

/

12 months

= _____ per month

This is your one-time, non-recurring monthly average.

Slow clap for doing the math. Picture a standing ovation in a packed theater. You're doing great.

Step 3: Add them together.

Grab your calculator. Add your fixed monthly expense number (plus) your one-time, non-recurring monthly average. What's the total?

For instance, let's say hypothetically it looks like this:

"Every month, I need $3,555 to cover my fixed monthly expenses. And my monthly average for one-time, non-recurring expenses is $2,113. So, $3,555 + $2,113 is $5,668."

This means $5,668 is the amount you must bring in the door every month to cover your total operating expenses.

Fixed monthly expenses _____

+

One-time expenses monthly average _____

=

Total monthly operating expenses _____

If your eyes are glazing over like a buttermilk donut, now is the time to... treat yourself to a donut. Or take a walk, play with your dog, hop onto your bike, blast your favorite song, or do something to boost your energy.

This is the point in the journey where every cell of your brain might be saying, "I just can't. This is too hard—too much math. My numbers are just awful. It's hopeless."

No. It is not hopeless, far from it. But you need to keep going. Take a break whenever you need to, but keep striding forward. Do not toss this book into the recycle bin and give up. You've already come too far to give up now! I'm asking you to place your trust in me and keep working your way through Chapters 11, 12, 13, and beyond.

Right now, the numbers might spell out a grim situation. But soon, the numbers are going to spell out your dream business and future. Keep marching.

CHAPTER 11:
Get Control of Your Payroll Expenses

By now, you know exactly how much revenue your business needs to generate each month in order to cover your total monthly operating expenses.

But what about payroll expenses? Let's look at this next.

> *Note: Even if you don't have any employees (aside from yourself) yet, read this chapter anyway. Because, sooner or later, you'll hire an assistant, receptionist, studio manager, another clinician or instructor, or all of the above. You can't do everything by yourself forever. It's not sustainable. So keep reading—even if you're a solopreneur for now. Plus, even if you're a one-woman operation, for the time being, you need to adjust your pricing so that it covers people you intend to hire in the future. More on this soon.*

Regarding your business, the people on your team are your most valuable asset. Think about it. If a hurricane wiped out your entire business—your office, studio, clinic, or shop was smashed to smithereens—you could rebuild again (even better than before) because of the people you've got on your team. You could move to another location and start up again from scratch because you've got the right people. Never forget that.

Without the people who work for you, your business would be DOA. So your payroll expense is essential to running a successful business. Otherwise, you'll be left to run your business as a one-woman show. That's not only unsustainable, but it is also downright unhealthy.

Take it from me. When I was out of commission for several weeks recovering from meningitis, if I didn't have a team in place to continue business as usual—shoutout to Shelley, my right-hand woman at the studio during that time—my business would have immediately crashed and burned. Or when I had my first baby, if I didn't have Flo—my studio's lead instructor, who stepped up to run operations in my absence—I wouldn't have been able to take maternity leave. Or if Barbara hadn't been promoted to full-time manager—allowing me to walk away from the daily operations and focus 100% of my energy on growing the business—I would not have been able to sell it for 40 times my original investment.

To Shelley, Flo, and Barbara: I love you, and I could not have done it without you. Thank you from the bottom of my heart.

Needless to say—but I'm going to say it anyway—your payroll expense is probably your most important expense. It is THE expense that allows you to grow. I almost hate to call it an "expense." A more accurate term would be "necessity" or "investment"—an investment that directly affects the prosperity of your business.

35% IS THE GOAL

In Chapter 9: Do a Profit Analysis, I explained that your payroll expense margin should be no more than 35% of your gross revenue.

Meaning, if your revenue is $100,000 per year, then your payroll expenses should be no more than $35,000.

If revenue is $200,000 annually, then payroll should be no more than $70,000. If revenue is $1,000,000 annually (yay, you!), then payroll should be no more than $350,000. And so on.

35% is a healthy margin for which to aim for most service-based businesses. One exception is online-based businesses. If you run an online-based business—you sell services online, work virtually, meet with clients on Zoom, and don't rent a physical location like a studio or shop—then, most likely, your operating expenses are extremely low. Since you pay very little in operating expenses, you can afford to have a payroll expense margin that's higher than 35% and still maintain a 30% profit margin.

But if you run a brick-and-mortar business such as a med spa, Pilates studio, boutique gym, eyelash extension studio, massage and wellness clinic, law practice with a physical location, chiropractic practice, that sort of thing, then 35% is a good target to aim for.

Right now, your payroll expense margin might be way higher than 35%. Like, WAY more. You might be thinking, "Erin, I know my payroll expense margin is high, but there's no way I can reduce how much I'm paying my staff. If I cut their pay, they will leave."

Which is exactly why you will not—I repeat, NOT—be decreasing your staff's pay. Absolutely not! Instead, you're going to increase your revenue so that you can pay everyone generously while still maintaining a 35% payroll margin and 30% profit margin. Repeat after me: "Increase, not decrease!"

But before you worry about increasing your revenue, first you need to know how much it costs you to maintain your staff and pay them what they're worth—because, just like you, they are worthy and deserving of being compensated fairly and living their best lives too.

Once you know exactly how much you need to cover payroll expenses, you're going to bake these expenses into your pricing so that it's all covered auto-magically.

CALCULATE YOUR PAYROLL EXPENSES

Now's the time to calculate how much monthly revenue you need to cover your payroll expenses. Remember, your payroll expenses include everything paid to your staff—employees and contractors—and yourself.

To make your life easier, so that you don't have to flip back to Chapter 9 searching for what's included, here is that list again.

Payroll expenses include:

- Gross wages (total compensation paid by the business before employment taxes withholding)

- Employer-matched payroll taxes for social security and Medicare
- 401K contributions paid by the business
- Employer-sponsored health insurance
- Paid time off
- Your owner's salary

CONTRACTORS

Let's start with contractors, also known as freelancers.

Your contractor wages are the easiest to tally because you don't have to include taxes or benefits paid by the business. It's simply the total compensation agreed upon and paid to the contractor on an hourly, monthly, or project basis. Some examples include:

- Makeup artist at your salon: flat rate of $75 per makeup application
- Virtual assistant for your coaching business: monthly retainer of $1,200 per month for up to 40 hours per month
- Guest instructor at your studio: $5,000 for a three-month teacher training program

Some businesses only work with contractors, so their contractor expenses are fixed—think back to your fixed monthly operating expenses—meaning you pay the contractor the same amount, or close to the same amount, each month.

A boutique fitness studio is a great example of this because most of the instructors who teach at one studio teach at other studios too. These contracted instructors determine their availability, manage their client schedules, and teach using their own methodology. And at the end of each month, they bill the studio for their total hours taught, which is usually right around the same amount month after month.

Other businesses use contractors sporadically. For instance, maybe you hire a diversity and inclusion coach to work with your team for three months to facilitate positive intergroup interaction in your office. It's a one-time payment of $4,000, not a recurring dealio.

If you live in the United States, at the end of each tax year, you send each contractor a 1099-Misc form that states, "This is how much I paid you in the last year." You don't submit their income taxes to the IRS on their behalf, nor do you pay into social security or Medicare. The contractor is responsible for reporting their income to the IRS and paying whatever taxes they owe.

So how much money do you pay to contractors in one year? If you're not sure, go find out. Clear your schedule for a day. Rummage through all the invoices you paid. Look at your bank statements. Make a list and total it up. As the owner, this is crucial information you need to know.

Total annual contractor expense

_____

EMPLOYEES

Employees can be part-time or full-time. These folks aren't self-employed. You employ them. Most likely, they work for you exclusively, which means you have their full attention. They're not juggling 12 other clients plus you. They can bring their whole mind, heart, and genius to your business. They might work for you 10, 20, or 30 hours a week, or more, depending on what you've agreed upon.

Depending on the laws in your city, state, or country, you might be responsible for paying their salary, as well as other benefits like health insurance.

If you live in the United States, at the end of each tax year, you send each employee a W-2 form that states, "This is how much I paid you in the last year." This form also shows the amount that got withheld for their income taxes and the amount paid to social security and Medicare.

So how much money do you pay to employees in one year? If you're not sure, let's find out.

Remember: YOU are an employee of your own company, too, but for this exercise only you are NOT going to include your owner's salary. We are going to tackle that in the next section.

If you use a payroll system like Justworks, Gusto, or QuickBooks, you can easily find the total. Log in. Run a report. Enter the date range you want (make sure it's for one year). Bingo. The system will tell you what you've paid.

Total gross wages   _____

+

Employer-matched payroll taxes   _____

+

401K contributions paid by the business   _____

+

Employer-sponsored health insurance   _____

=

Total annual employee expense   _____

YOUR OWNER'S PAY

In Chapter 9: Do a Profit Analysis, I mentioned that your owner's salary should be included in your payroll expense. And I emphasized that you absolutely—without question—should be paying yourself an owner's salary. In fact, your salary should be the first item on the payroll list.

"Yes, Erin," you reply, as spoken by an adolescent teenager annoyed with her parents.

Suppose you're already paying yourself an owner's salary; hats off to you! Even if the amount you're paying yourself is peanuts, at least you're in the habit of paying yourself something. That's a start.

But I don't want you to merely earn peanuts. I want you to earn enough money to create the life of your dreams.

WHAT IS YOUR DREAM?

Let me ask you, what is your dream life? What do you truly want? I'm asking you to dream big and don't hold back. Because whatever you want, it is attainable.

Do you want to own a home? Or a second home that you can rent out as an income-generating property?

Do you want a specific car? A boat? A vacation house in France? (Yes, ma'am! That's my personal dream. I've already picked out the exact patio furniture I want while I'm basking in the dreamy golden light, sipping sauvignon blanc, surrounded by vineyards in Sancerre!)

Do you want to pay for your kids' gymnastics classes, piano lessons, and soccer club?

Do you want to stash money away for retirement, or your kids' college educations?

Do you want to have date night with your husband once a week at a lovely restaurant?

Do you want to install a pool in your backyard, renovate your master bathroom, or build an extension to your house?

Do you want to travel multiple times a year and stay in the nicest rooms at the nicest resorts? (Me again. This is what I want!)

Do you want to buy a condo for your elderly mom, or help your kids make a down payment on their first home one day?

All of these things cost money. That money has to come from somewhere— and that somewhere is your business.

Right now, you might feel like the life you want is incredibly far away. You're thinking, "I want to own a home, get a new car, obliterate all of my debt, travel the world, yes to all of that!" But these visions might feel wildly unrealistic or waaa-aaay off in the distant future. Especially if you're barely breaking even (or you're in the negative zone) with your business—right now these goals might feel like preposterous fantasies.

Here's what I want you to remember. *Dreams do come true.* Billions of people own a home. You can too. Billions of people take vacations. You can too. Everything you want is doable. You can achieve what you want, and it's going to happen in gradual stages. You might have a -20% profit margin right now, but then you do an overhaul and bring it to 0% and then 5% and then 10% and eventually 30%. Before you know it, you're leading an entirely different life! It will not happen overnight, but it can happen over time.

All the dreams you have for your life are possible and can come from your business—as long as you include this money in your owner's salary and bake it into your pricing.

> *I use the word bake a lot for somebody who does not bake or cook—seriously. I'm literally the worst in the kitchen. I might suck at baking muffins, but I love baking a profit into your business model!*

WHAT'S YOUR DREAM NUMBER?

Here's my next question for you: What's your dream number?

Meaning, how much is this dream life going to cost you each year? That's what you're about to calculate.

Start by totaling all your *personal annual expenses*—the amount it costs you to maintain your current lifestyle. Your mortgage, car payment, electricity, water, food bill, and so on. Add it up. That's the bare minimum amount you need to pay yourself to maintain your current situation. Let's say it's $70,000. Cool. Consider this your personal *break-even number.* You need to pay yourself $70,000 per year to keep rolling with your current life.

Next, add exciting things that you don't have *yet*—but *want.* Add dance classes for the kids, a personal trainer, a meal delivery service, a landscape artist who transforms your backyard into a serene oasis, a weekly blowout at the hair salon, charitable donations to a great cause, or whatever your dream life would include. Google to figure out approximately how much each new thing would cost. Let's say, hypothetically, that all of these new additions would cost an additional $50,000 per year. Your break-even number was $70,000. Add $50,000. That's $120,000. Okay, that's your *dream number*. You need to pay yourself $120,000 per year to afford your dream life. This is your dream salary.

Personal annual expenses   _____

+

Annual "wants"   _____

=

Annual dream salary   _____

It's important to know your dream number. It gives you something specific to aim for. Every woman's situation is unique. You might be able to hit your dream number next month! Or climbing up to that point might take a year or two (or more). But you can get there. And damn, it feels good once you do.

FIND YOUR MONTHLY AVERAGE

Take the total amount you pay to contractors in one year.

Take the total amount you pay to employees in one year.

And then take your dream salary—the amount you need in order to afford your dream life.

Add these three numbers together. Divide by 12.

This gives you a monthly average. That's how much money you need each month to cover payroll expenses.

For example, $40,000 (contractors) + $90,000 (employees) + $138,000 (dream salary) = $268,000.

$268,000 divided by 12 is $22,333.33.

So, you need $22,333.33 each month to cover payroll expenses, including paying yourself an excellent salary.

Total annual contractor expense   _____

+

Total annual employee expense   _____

+

Total annual owner's dream salary   _____

=

Total annual payroll expense   _____

/

12 months

=

Monthly payroll expense   _____

NO TEAM (YET)

What if you currently don't have a staff and are starring in your one-woman show? Honey, it's time to imagine your dream team and figure out exactly how much it will cost to have the team you want. Because the last thing you want to happen is being in a position where you absolutely need to hire somebody but you don't have enough money to do so.

Maybe your business won't go from a one-woman show to a full-out Broadway musical with an ensemble cast of 50. But it can at least become a duet or trio.

A little bit of trivia for you. Theater professionals raised me. My mom is a professional director and actress, and my dad was a technical director and playwright. I grew up on stage and even majored in musical theater in college, hence all of the musical references. But I digress.

If you are the only employee in your business for now, here's your next step:

Figure out how much it would cost to add just *one* team member.

Maybe you contract a virtual assistant for a few hours weekly to take over some administrative tasks. Maybe you hire a part-time employee who can start taking on some clients each month. It doesn't have to be a full-time, salaried employee with paid vacation, health insurance, and a 401K. But whatever role it is, now is the time to determine how much it's going to cost your business so that you can bake it into your pricing. That way, when the time comes, you'll have the cash in your account ready to roll! You will be able to afford the addition.

Here's an example. Imagine that you are ready to hire a part-time front desk person to greet your clients and check them in for their facial appointments when they walk in the door. This person will also be responsible for answering the phone, responding to client emails, and selling your skin care products when clients checkout.* You decide that you will pay this person $20 per hour and you would like for her to work 10 hours per week, which is 40 hours per month.

$20 per hour x 40 hours per month = $800 per month

Cool. Knowing this, you can bake $800 per month into your new-and-improved pricing model. That way, you're socking this cash away, saving up, month after month. When the moment arrives and you're ready to hire this delightful assistant, you've got the cash ready![1] You can do it. No problemo.

Let's recap. In this chapter, you learned how much your payroll costs each month—or how much it will eventually cost—so that you can set your pricing

---

1   *This fabulous new receptionist will probably sell so many products, she'll pay for her own salary plus more! This is a must-do.*

to prepare for the future you want. Overhauling your prices today gives you the financial power to do exciting things in the future.

CHAPTER 12:

Calculate Your Monthly Revenue Needs

Many new business owners open their doors and expect not to make money for their first couple of years in business. They go into business expecting, "I probably won't be able to pay myself for a while. I may even lose money. But that's just the way it goes. That's showbiz, baby!"

According to *Forbes,* most new businesses don't generate a profit for 18 to 24 months. (Aklap, 2015)

But what if I told you that you do *not* have to lose money your first couple of years in business—and, in fact, you can pay yourself from day one?

You absolutely can.

When opening a business, the goal is to make money as quickly as possible. Your business doesn't technically start making money until you've paid everything else. That "everything else" is considered your business' monthly break-even. You want to reach your break-even as soon as possible. Once you break even, then you can move into the next phase and become profitable.

In this chapter, I will show you how to calculate your monthly break-even—the bare minimum your business needs to generate in revenue each month to operate without losing money—and how to calculate your monthly revenue needs *with* profit baked in. Once you've calculated this number, you can establish appropriate pricing for your business.

Your monthly break-even includes all operating expenses (which you calculated in Chapter 10), all payroll expenses (which you totaled up in Chapter 11), and, remember, payroll includes your owner's salary too.

As an owner-operator, *you must pay yourself,* and you should be paying yourself from day one! Contrary to popular belief, a business owner should not pay herself last. She should pay herself first because there would be no business without her!

"That sounds wonderful, Erin," you might be thinking, "but the reality is, my business is barely making enough right now to keep the electricity on, let alone pay myself."

To which I say, "That's exactly why you need to overhaul your pricing. You need to bake your ideal salary into your pricing model (which, in some instances, might mean raising your prices significantly) so that you can get paid, pronto."

If you're not paying yourself, then you are not truly running a business. You're running an expensive hobby or volunteer project. And I know that's *not* why you went into business for yourself.

"But how much should I pay myself?" you might wonder.

To which I would reply, "We just calculated your dream salary in the previous chapter."

But if you're currently not paying yourself at all, paying yourself your dream salary might feel like an impossible leap.

You've got to start somewhere, so I want you to think about everything you do inside your business. Make a list and detail every single task you perform and the time it takes you to complete each task. How much would you expect to be compensated if you were to do this job for another company? Whatever that figure is, that's the amount you should be paying yourself.

However, with a capital H! Calculating your owner's salary this way can be a trap—because, as we learned in Part One of this book, women tend to undervalue themselves grossly. You might come up with a lowball salary because you don't recognize what you actually deserve.

A better question might be, if you were to hire a man to do your job right now—this man would take over 100% of your responsibilities and hours—how much would you have to pay him?

$60,000?
$75,000?
$100,000 or more?

Whatever that salary is, that's how much you should be paying yourself at the very least. You must include your owner's salary in your business' monthly break-even.

Let's assume you landed on $60,000 per year. (For now, anyway, because you'll certainly give yourself a raise in the future.) Take $60,000 and divide it by 12 months. You need to bake that $5,000 per month into your pricing. Because without you doing your job, the business would cease to exist.

Another way to determine your salary is simply to ask yourself, "How much do I want my salary to be? What's my dream salary?" (I walked you through this exercise in the previous chapter.) As an entrepreneur, ultimately, your salary is whatever you decide it's going to be.

HOW TO DETERMINE YOUR MONTHLY BREAK-EVEN

Add your total monthly operating expenses + total monthly payroll expenses (including your owner's salary) and what have you got? Whatever the number is, that's your monthly break-even. This is the cash you need each month to keep your business open and everyone paid.

Let's pretend you got $10,000, just for simple math. That means that, at the very least, your business needs to generate $10,000 in revenue each month to break even.

Monthly operating expenses (Chapter 10) _____

\+

Monthly payroll expenses (Chapter 11) _____

=

Monthly break-even _____

Once you break even, the goal is to become profitable.

If you remember from Chapter 9: Do a Profit Analysis, the standard benchmark for service-based businesses is a 30% profit margin. So we want to add a 30% profit margin to the monthly break-even you just calculated.

Here's how you do this.

Subtract

Subtract 30% from 100%.

100% - 30% = 70%

70% represents the percentage of monthly revenue that comes from your break-even.

Convert

Convert 70% into a decimal.

70 divided by 100 = 0.7

Try out these steps. But this time, plug in your own business numbers.

Monthly break-even _____
/
0.70
=
Monthly revenue needed with 30% profit _____

ONE STEP AT A TIME

You may have had a rude awakening in Chapter 9: Do a Profit Analysis. You might've calculated that your current profit margin is actually negative. You're losing money each month.

If you find yourself in this position, it's okay and totally to be expected. Step one is you're going to aim for break-even. That's the first goal you want to hit. Once you break even, your goal might be to bake in a 5% profit margin, then 10%, then 20%, ultimately reaching 30% (and beyond).

It's unrealistic to think you will go from a negative profit margin to a 30% profit margin overnight. It's a gradual rise to the top, but once you roll out your new pricing, you'll arrive at 30% before you know it. Hello, vacation home in France, here we coooo-ooome!

CHAPTER 13:

Calculate Your Monthly Client Capacity

By now, you've done several Badass Math Ninja calculations.

You know your current operating expenses, payroll expenses, and your dream owner's salary.

You know exactly how much your business must make monthly to break even.

And you know how much your business needs to make each month to have a profit—ideally a 30% profit margin, at minimum.

Pop the Champagne because you've already accomplished so much! Figuring out those numbers is a major step forward. However, as you're sipping that chilled glass of bubbly, you may wonder, "Uhhh, so, how am I going to make that much money every month?!!" You might be feeling nervous rather than celebratory.

Here's what I want you to know:

Whatever amount you need to generate to secure your 30% profit margin— whether it's $10,000 per month or $50,000 or $100,000 or more—you can get there. Other women have done this. You can do this too. And the next step on the journey from "here" to "there" is to calculate your client capacity.

"My client what now?"

Your *client capacity* is the total number of clients that you (or you and your team) can comfortably serve within a given period of time: week, month, or year.

For instance, maybe you're a solo practitioner and you can only serve five clients per week because it's just you. Or maybe you own a full-service spa with multiple employees, so your business can serve a total of 100 clients per week. It all depends! Every business (and every woman) is different.

We'll figure out your client capacity—together—right now.

Right off the bat, you might assume, "Well, I'm supposed to work 40 hours per week. Therefore, my client capacity is...however many clients I can squeeze into those 40 hours."

Nope! That's not how we're going to calculate your client capacity. The question is not "How many people can I cram into a given period of time?" The real question is "What is my *ideal* schedule and life?"

Remember when I asked you to dream up your ideal owner's salary? No holds barred.

I want you to do the same thing right now—but instead of envisioning your dream salary, I want you to think about your dream schedule.

WHAT IS YOUR DREAM SCHEDULE?

Do you ever come across something that is completely janky and poorly designed and wonder, "Who came up with this shit? This is stupid!" That's how I feel about the 40-hour workweek.

If you live in the United States, where it's standard to work 40 hours per week and 50 weeks per year (honey, this is no way to live), then you probably assume, "I need to work 40 hours a week. That's just how it is." As a self-employed woman, you may think, "If I need to work 50 or 60 hours a week, so be it! That's the price I pay for the joy of being my own boss. I have to do whatever it takes."

And you probably think to yourself, "I need to cram every single hour of my day with clients. That's the goal. Free space—fill it with paying clients!

Monetize every minute! The more people I can fit into the day, the better."

I challenge you to think differently. I want you to think more European-ly (I just made up that word. I should trademark it!), with visions of daily two-hour siestas, leisurely dinners by candlelight, unhurried holidays in the sun, and summer sabbaticals in Barcelona flooding your brain!

Pretend for a moment that the typical 40-hour workweek literally doesn't exist. Nobody does that. It's not the norm. Or to stretch things further, pretend that working 40 hours a week is actually *illegal.* You'll face a hefty fine if you do it. It is not allowed. You must work less.

If working 40 hours a week was NOT an option, how would you rebuild your schedule?

Here's a really exciting question to consider:

If you could build your dream schedule, what would it be?

Would you only work Monday through Friday from 9 a.m. to 2 p.m. while your kids are in school?

Would you only work four days per week so that you always have a three-day weekend? (Think 52 additional days off every year.)

Would you only work seasonally—say, during the winter months when the snowbirds are in town? (Can you tell I live in South Florida where the state's population doubles during winter when the snowbirds return to their winter homes in the sun?)

You may want two months of vacation time each year rather than a paltry two weeks.

What is your ideal work schedule? Dream it up! Because whatever it is, we will bake it into your pricing.

NEED SOME INSPIRATION?

Here's the work schedule I dreamed up for myself—and, thanks to math, made a reality.

- Birthday break during the first two weeks of the year. My birthday is January 7th. This year, I took a solo 10-day trip to France to celebrate.

- Work mid-January through mid-March.

- Spring break with my kids! Where are we going this year? (In the last few years, we visited the Blue Ridge Mountains, St. Augustine, Orlando, and the Ichetucknee River.)

- Work late-March through Memorial Day, which is the end of May here in the United States.

- Summer break with my kids! I call it Mommy Summer Camp, and it's a fucking blast. This year, we're making an international trip: family safari in Tanzania; here we come!

- Work mid-August through mid-November.

- Thanksgiving break with my family. An entire week of eating, drinking, and more eating! My favorite! (Notice how I did not include cooking in this itinerary?)

- Work the first two weeks in December.

- Winter break is the rest of the year.

I work anywhere from 39 to 42 weeks a year—depending on where I'm traveling and when my kids are off from school. I take at least 10 weeks of vacation each year; honestly, you should too. This is entirely doable once you get your pricing dialed in correctly and stop overworking and underearning.

When I *am* working, this is my schedule.

MONDAY: ADMIN DAY

6 a.m.   Wake up and get my kids ready for school.

7:15 a.m.   Take my kids to school. (We usually sing-along to Kidz Bop Radio in the car! If I have to hear "We Don't Talk About Bruno" one more time, though, I swear I might spontaneously combust.)

8 a.m.   Personal training session.

9 a.m.   Breakfast on my patio (lately, my favorite is an egg sunny-side-up, toast, sliced tomato, and grated Gruyère cheese).

9:30 a.m.   Loooooooooong shower or bath with aromatherapy products, salt scrub, all the things.

11 a.m.   Private French lesson (yes, notice that I allowed myself 1.5 hours to shower, putz around, and primp myself! It's more than a shower. It's a lifestyle!)

12-2 p.m.   Admin time to work on my business. I don't meet with clients on Mondays. Instead, I do other tasks, including bookkeeping, marketing, writing, meeting with my business coach, etc.

2 p.m.   Leave to pick up my kids from school. My work day is done.

TUESDAY, WEDNESDAY, THURSDAY: CLIENT DAYS

6 a.m.   Wake up and get my kids ready for school.

7:15 a.m.   Take my kids to school (I cherish these car-ride moments because it's when we listen to music, talk about what they're studying, laugh, and goof around together).

8 a.m.   Personal training session either solo or with my husband joining in!

9 a.m.	Breakfast on my patio.
9:30 a.m.	Another deliciously lengthy shower, aka me time.
10 a.m. - 2 p.m.	Make myself available to clients: Zoom meetings, answer emails, reply to audio messages on Voxer, comfort clients who are having a money-anxiety-meltdown, and help clients overhaul their pricing and their lives!
2 p.m.	Leave to pick up my kids from school. Work = donezo.

FRI-YAY: WHATEVER THE FUCK I WANT TO DO DAY

6 a.m.	Wake up and get my kids ready for school.
7:15 a.m.	Take my kids to school.
8 a.m.	Personal training session (yes, I work out five days a week—primarily for my mental health. Although toned shoulders and a peach-shaped booty are a nice bonus.)
9 a.m.	Post-workout breakfast with my gym friends (no shower, we're stinky and proud of it).
11 a.m.	Private French lesson. (Determined to become fluent and fool people into thinking I am a native-born Parisian! After all, my maiden name *is* Blanchette).
12-2 p.m.	Whatever I want! Bubble bath, therapy, facial, mani/pedi, lunch with a friend, doctor appointment, or…write a book!
2 p.m.	Leave to pick up my kids from school. The work week is over—time for weekend vibes.

SATURDAY AND SUNDAY: FAMILY TIME!

We splash around in the pool, hit the beach, peruse Target (seriously, I cannot be trusted in this store), host cookouts in our backyard with friends, and have dinner at an oceanfront tiki bar (one of the many benefits of living in South Florida), or whatever we feel like doing.

Notice how I don't cram every single available minute with "work?" Hell no! I leave enough space in my schedule to savor the day and live my life. Let me tell you, it's during those moments of open space (that 90-minute shower and primping session, puttering around the house, or sipping wine on the patio) when I get my best business ideas.

Space creates *more* money. A hectic schedule and tons of stress creates *less* money. I promise you that.

MAX CAPACITY IS *NOT* THE GOAL

During the time when I make myself available to clients—which happens on Tuesday, Wednesday, and Thursday, for 12 hours per week—I don't want to cram those hours with back-to-back client meetings, which means that I don't want to work at 100% capacity. I prefer to operate at 50% capacity.

I want to leave 30 minutes in between client calls so that I can fully prepare for the next meeting and be present with each person. Plus, I want to take a lunch break because you don't want to talk to me when I'm hangry!

Because I'm giving myself breaks in between sessions, my actual time spent interacting with clients (meetings, calls, etc.) is roughly two hours per day, three days per week. That comes out to six hours per week.

EXAMPLE: MY PERSONAL CLIENT CAPACITY

If I'm only available six hours per week and I only want to work 40 weeks per year, that means I am available to work with clients a total of 240 hours per year. Here's the math:

---

6 hours per week x 40 weeks per year = 240 hours per year

240 hours per year is my personal *work capacity.*

What's the average per month? To find out, I just need to divide by 12.

240 hours per year / 12 months = 20 hours per month

Remember in a previous chapter when I said I work an average of 20 hours per month? Now, you can see how I arrived at that number.

Knowing that I only have the capacity—in my dream schedule—to work 20 hours per month, how many clients can I accommodate?

To find out, I divide 20 hours per month by the average number of hours that my clients meet with me per month.

On average, my clients meet with me for two hours per month. This is my *monthly client utilization.* On average, each client utilizes two hours of my time every month.

This means that I'm only available to serve ten clients per month.

How did I determine that?

> I take my average working hours per month (20 hours) and divide by my monthly client utilization (two hours).
>
> 20 / 2 = 10
>
> This means I can serve ten clients per month—while still maintaining my dream schedule.

Ta-da! Ten clients per month is my personal *client capacity.*

Do you see how I arrived at that number?

Now it's your turn.

CALCULATE YOUR CLIENT CAPACITY

Step 1: Write out your dream schedule.

Decide how many weeks per year you want to work. Maybe it's 25, 30, or 42, or something else.

> Dream weeks per year = _____

Decide how many hours per week you want to work. It could be 2 hours or 20 hours or 31 or whatever you desire. Hey, this is your dream!

Get honest with yourself about what your dream schedule really is. If you could have anything, what would it be?

Dream hours per week = _____

Step 2: Calculate your dream working hours per year.

Multiply the total number of hours per week that you want to work by how many weeks per year you wish to work.

For instance, perhaps you want to work 18 hours per week x 40 weeks a year.

18 x 40 = 720

This means that in your dream schedule, you will be working 720 hours per year.

Dream weeks per year _____
x
Dream hours per week _____
=
Dream hours per year _____

Step 3: Find your dream monthly average.

Divide total number of hours per year by 12 months.

To continue the previous example, let's do 720 divided by 12.

720 / 12 = 60

This means, in your dream schedule, you'd be working around 60 hours per month on average.

Dream hours per year _____ / 12 months
=
Dream average monthly hours _____

Step 4: Find your current monthly client utilization.

Take the total number of hours you worked in the last full month (or the total number of sessions conducted) and divide it by the total number of clients you serviced in the last full month. That's how you find your *current monthly client utilization.*

For example, let's say you're a massage therapist.

If you completed 90 massages last month and you saw 60 clients, you would do 90 divided by 60.

90 / 60 = 1.5

Your monthly client utilization is 1.5. That means, on average, your clients schedule massages with you 1.5 times per month. Another way to phrase this is: a typical client will utilize 1.5 sessions from you every month.

Current hours worked per month _____
/
Current number of clients _____
=
Current monthly client utilization _____

But let's say you do NOT want to do 90 massages per month because that's way too damn many and your poor hands are aching! Let's say, in your dream schedule, you would only do 60 massages per month.

Step 5: Find your ideal monthly client capacity.

You know that your clients typically book 1.5 massages per month (this is your current monthly client utilization). And you've decided that you want to do 60 massages per month (that's your ideal schedule).

Take 60 massages per month and divide that by your monthly client utilization of 1.5 to find your ideal monthly client capacity.

$60 / 1.5 = 40$

This means 40 clients per month is your ideal monthly client capacity.

Forty is the total number of clients you can comfortably serve each month while still maintaining your dream schedule and doing the amount of work that you wish to do (not more!).

Dream average monthly hours (Step 3) _____
/
Current monthly client utilization (Step 4) _____
=
_____ ideal monthly client capacity

Confetti burst! And *that* is how you figure out your ideal monthly client capacity.

What do you actually want?

It all comes down to one question: *What is your dream business and life?*

Are you someone who loves to run a bustling shop with multiple employees and clients rolling in and out all throughout the day? You get energized by seeing lots of faces each day, you love the banter and conversation, and you thrive on this energy? If so, great! You can design your business accordingly.

Or maybe the opposite is true. Maybe you're very introverted and your dream situation would be to serve three clients per month. You can't really handle dealing with hoards of people. You prefer intimacy and exclusivity. You can do that. For instance, there are chefs, trainers, and massage therapists who only work with a tiny handful of high-end clients each month—that's certainly a thing you can do! For every personality, there is a pricing model that can work—and that will provide the income you want. But first, you have to be honest with yourself about what your dream really is.

You may be wondering, "But wait, Erin. I'm not a massage therapist. I don't really do 'sessions' with clients as a massage therapist does. My business isn't like that at all." Maybe you're a copywriter or virtual assistant or you run a spa and have a team that serves clients.

Let's look at a few more examples of calculating your monthly client capacity for different professions and scenarios.

COPYWRITER

This is one of my favorite examples because I recently worked with a copywriter to help her overhaul her pricing. Since our work together—less than a year ago—her business has skyrocketed, and she's cut her workload in half!

Now, calculating her monthly client capacity got a wee bit tricky because this copywriter doesn't really work by the hour or by the session. Instead, she sells packages based on the number of pieces she will write for a client.

For instance, she might say to a client, "I can write ten blog posts for your company for X dollars," or, "I can write 50 social media blurbs for Y dollars." I asked her, "So how long does it take you to complete each package you sell?" She told me (with a heavy sigh), "It varies!" And therein lies the difficulty.

As she explained it, "It doesn't take me the exact same amount of time to write every piece. Sometimes I can write a piece for a client in no time when inspiration hits. I could write one blog post in 20 minutes! But other times, it takes me longer if I experience writer's block or if it's a particularly challenging project requiring more time to think. That same blog post might take me one to two hours to complete."

"Okay," I responded. "On average, how many hours per week do you dedicate to writing?"

"Twenty, maybe?" she guessed.

"Got it," I said. "On average, you dedicate 20 hours of writing time each week to your clients. That sounds like a lot! Is this how many hours you would like to be writing a week?"

She replied immediately, "No." And continued, "I would prefer no more than three hours a day of writing. After that, my brain is fried. And, if I'm dreaming up my ideal schedule, I would prefer only to write four days a week."

Do you know what I did next? I took the three hours a day and multiplied it by four days per week to give us 12 hours per week of writing time. Twelve hours per week is her dream schedule.

Next, my client decided that she only wanted to work 42 weeks a year (the 10 weeks of vacation trend has really spread like wildfire among my clients), so I multiplied 42 weeks per year by 12 hours per week to get 504 hours per year.

42 x 12 = 504 hours per year

This copywriter would like to work 504 hours per year. That's her ideal schedule. Divide that number by 12 to find the monthly average.

504 hours per year / 12 months = 42 hours per month

On average, this lovely copywriter would like to work 42 hours monthly. Sounds delightful to me!

Put a pin in this number because we're coming back to it.

Then, I asked my client to calculate her current monthly client utilization. Recall that she's currently writing 20 hours per week and working 50 weeks per year (you read that correctly—she was only giving herself two weeks of vacation per year before she and I started working together! What a nightmare!).

> 20 hours per week x 50 weeks = 1,000 hours per year
>
> Divide that by 12 to find the monthly average.
>
> 1,000 hours per year / 12 months = 83.33 hours per month (rounding to 83 to keep it simple)

So, on average, she's doing 83 hours of writing time each month. That's the current scenario. Within those 83 hours, she typically serves 15 clients each month. "How does it feel to work with 15 clients per month?" I inquired, already suspecting that the answer would be "Not good." And my hunch was correct. Fifteen felt way too overwhelming for her. Her brain was pulled in 15 different directions, and it was difficult to keep all the details straight. She didn't feel as if the quality of her writing was as good as she knew it could be because she was stretched too thin.

> Take 83 hours per month (how much she's currently writing for her clients) and divide it by 15 clients (total clients she currently services per month) to get 5.53.
>
> 83 / 15 = 5.53 monthly client utilization

On average, each client requires 5.53 hours of her time per month. Again, let's round that up to 6 hours per month to get a monthly client utilization of 6 hours per month—and to pad her schedule with a little more downtime.

"Next," I said, "We're going to calculate your *new* monthly client capacity for your *new* dream schedule." (Picture me: gleefully rubbing my hands together!)

Remember, her dream schedule includes 42 hours of writing time per month. So, I took 42 and divided it by her monthly client utilization of 6 to get 7 clients per month.

42 hours per month / 6 monthly client utilization = 7 ideal monthly client capacity

"Okay, buttercup! In your dream schedule, you are working 42 hours per month. On average, each client utilizes 6 hours of your time each month. This means, in your dream scenario, you have the capacity to serve 7 clients per month," I told her, summing it all up.

Hearing this math laid out, she felt nervous, excited, and, most of all, *relieved*. Seven clients sounded way more doable than 15. Over the next six months, she rolled out her new pricing, decreased her workload by almost half, and doubled her monthly revenue!

The best part? She felt even prouder about the work she was delivering. In a follow-up chat, she told me, "Because I'm serving fewer clients, I can bring each client my full attention, and the quality of my writing has improved. My clients are getting the 'best' of me, not a fried and overwhelmed version of me."

More money, more free time, and higher quality services too? Just another day in the life of a Pricing Overhaul® coach. All we need now is a vacation to the Loire Valley of France and my work here is done…which we actually made happen when I hired this copywriter client of mine to conduct a writing workshop at the Luxury in Business Retreat™ I hosted in Sancerre, France! (Dreams do come true!)

Let's look at one more example of how to calculate your monthly client capacity. This time, we'll look at a business that has multiple employees, not just one.

SPA

Let's imagine that you run a business that employs multiple people. For instance, you're a spa owner with a team in place. You offer multiple services to your clients. Each service has a different time duration (perhaps one service is 30 minutes, another is 90 minutes, and so on). You might be puzzled by how you calculate your monthly client capacity, because not every client is coming in for the same service requiring the same amount of time.

In this case, you will need to calculate your monthly client capacity for each individual service type. I'm going to show you an example of how to do that.

If you own a spa that offers facials, waxing, and reflexology, you will first need to determine how many hours per month your entire team is available for each service. Look at your spa's schedule and calculate the following.

Facials

There are five estheticians with a combined total availability of 50 hours each week.

Your spa is open 52 weeks a year, although you personally don't want to work all 52 weeks.

50 hours per week x 52 weeks per year = 2,600 hours per year

2,600 / 12 months = 216.66 hours per month. Again, for simple math, we're rounding it down to 216.

You determine that your monthly client utilization is currently 1, meaning your clients typically come in 1 time per month for facials.

Next, you take the total number of hours available per month, which is 216, and you divide it by your monthly client utilization of 1, which means that your monthly client capacity for facials is 216 clients.

216 / 1 = 216

Waxing

There are two wax technicians with a combined total availability of 20 hours each week.

Your spa is open 52 weeks a year.

20 hours per week x 52 weeks per year = 1,040 hours per year

1,040 / 12 months = 86.66 hours per month. We're going to round that down to 86.

But! For your spa, wax appointments aren't 1 hour each. They schedule in 30-minute increments, so if there are 86 hours per month available, your business can accommodate 172 wax appointments monthly.

86 hours x 2 appointments per hour = 172 appointments available per month

You determine that your monthly client utilization is currently 1.25.

Next, you take the total number of appointments available per month, which is 172, and you divide it by your monthly client utilization of 1.25, which means that your monthly client capacity for wax clients is 137.6.

172 / 1.25 = 137.6

Again, you're not going to have a 0.6 client, so I round down—always rounding down to give your business and your staff a little breathing room—to 137, which means that your monthly client capacity for wax clients is 137.

Reflexology

There is one reflexologist at your spa. In fact, this is a new service you recently added to your menu. She is only available 20 hours a week, and she negotiated a compensation package that included two weeks of paid vacation, plus one week of paid sick leave, so she's available to see clients 49 weeks a year.

20 hours a week x 49 weeks a year = 980 hours per year

980 / 12 months = 81.66 hours per month

Because this is a new service, you don't have a current monthly client utilization, so you ask the reflexologist how frequently she recommends that clients should come in each month. She tells you that two sessions per month provide the best results, so you decide to go with two as your monthly client utilization.

Next, you take the total number of hours that she's available (81) and divide it by the intended monthly client utilization (2) to get 40.5.

$$81 / 2 = 40.5$$

Since you already see the pattern here, you will round down to 40 to get a monthly client capacity of 40 reflexology clients.

Is it a little more complicated to calculate monthly client capacity when you have a variety of services plus a team? Sure is! Is it impossible? Hell no! As you can see, it's just a matter of plugging numbers into the same formula to figure out your capacity for each individual service you offer. You're a smart and capable woman. You have conquered plenty of challenges in the past. You can do this, too.

BOTTOM LINE: YOUR MONTHLY CLIENT CAPACITY IS WHATEVER YOU DECIDE IT'S GOING TO BE

It might be serving two clients per month or 20 or 500, along with the support of your skilled team. What is your dream schedule? And, what is the client capacity that allows for that schedule to happen?

If you're still unsure, go back and read this chapter more slowly. Do the math and check it twice. When you're ready, head to the next chapter, and let's keep building out your dream business and life.

CHAPTER 14:
Calculate Your Monthly Client Value

Now…it's the moment you've been waiting for.

Imagine a big brass marching band standing by your desk, ready to play! Cue the drum roll!

All of the calculations you've done up until this point have prepared you for THIS magical moment.

The moment when you find out exactly how much each client should be paying you—aka your *monthly client value.*

What is your monthly client value?

In the last chapter, you figured out your monthly client capacity: how many clients you can comfortably serve each month while maintaining your dream schedule.

Once you know your monthly client capacity, you can calculate your monthly client value.

Your monthly client value is how much each client must be "worth" to your company to afford to have them as a client. By doing the math, you might realize that each new client needs to pay a minimum of $500 per month or $1,000 or $4,444, or whatever. Anything less and they're not worth your time! They're bogging down your schedule and holding you back from earning what you need.

You don't know your monthly client value?

No stress because we're about to figure it out together.

A WORD OF CAUTION: LOTS OF FEELS AHEAD

The math we're about to do might provoke some intense emotions. Because your monthly client value might be a LOT higher than what you currently charge. At this point in the journey, my clients often get bombarded with feelings of doubt and fear—followed by shame and embarrassment.

At this point, I usually hear my clients say one of two things:

"The math tells me I should be charging more, but I can't charge that much. My clients won't pay for that."

Or:

"I had no idea THAT'S how much I should have been charging all this time. I can't believe I've been undercharging that much. I've been leaving thousands of dollars on the table—money that could be sitting in my account right now. Uggggh."

Take a deep breath. Inhale through your nose. Exhale through your mouth. Lift your glass to your lips and take a big, healthy sip of wine. (Truth be told, I'm following my own advice right now before I continue writing the rest of this chapter.)

Whatever the math tells you, it's okay. You don't know what you don't know. Until you picked up this book, you did not know the formulas for calculating how much you should've been charging. Today, that all changes!

Are you ready to determine how much your clients should pay you?

Let's do the math—together.

CALCULATE YOUR IDEAL MONTHLY CLIENT VALUE

Back in Chapter 12, you calculated your *monthly revenue needed* with 30% profit baked in. I want you to go back to that chapter now and grab that number. This is the total of your operating expenses, payroll expenses, owner's salary, and profit (ideally 30%). In other words, the total amount of money your business needs to generate each month to cover all expenses, pay your team, pay yourself, AND generate a profit on top.

What is it? Write it down. You'll need that number in a sec.

From Chapter 12:
Monthly revenue needed with 30% profit =

_____

Okay, now reference back to your *monthly client capacity,* which you determined in Chapter 13. This is the total number of clients you can comfortably serve each month while adhering to your dream schedule.

What is it? Write it down again.

From Chapter 13:
Ideal monthly client capacity =

_____

I will now reveal the mind-blowingly simple formula that tells you exactly how much you should be charging. Are you ready?

Monthly revenue needed with 30% profit / ideal monthly client capacity = your ideal monthly client value

That's it! Hallelujah! Let the angels sing! All the math you've done has led you to this very simple formula. Let me say it again!

Monthly revenue needed with 30% profit / ideal monthly client capacity = your ideal monthly client value

I know. Can you believe how simple this is? Now you know exactly how much you need to be charging.

"But, Erin, can you show me an example?"

Oui, bien sûr! Yes, of course! (See, all those private French lessons have been paying off!)

EXAMPLE: PERSONAL CHEF

Let's imagine that you're a personal chef. You sell personalized meal plans that you prepare and deliver to your clients' homes. You craft each meal with love, heart, and organic kale to boot! You save your clients countless hours and make life easier for kitchen-challenged people (like myself!) so that their kids eat vegetables and do not starve!

For this example, let's say you calculated that your monthly revenue needed with 30% profit baked in is $10,000.

Your ideal monthly capacity for clients is 20.

That means that each client must be worth $500 per month to your business. How did we get there? Remember, here's the formula:

Monthly revenue needed with 30% profit / ideal monthly client capacity = your ideal monthly client value

> Here's that same formula with numbers plugged in:
>
> $10,000 / 20 = $500
>
> This means $500 is your ideal monthly client value.

This means, going forward, every client you serve needs to pay you $500 per month, on average, in order for you to have your dream revenue and dream schedule.

Of course, not every client will pay exactly $500 per month. You will probably have different plans at different price points—for example, five meals per week, ten meals per week, 20 meals per week, and so on. We'll get into how to build these types of packages in the next chapter. But $500 is the average that each client needs to pay per month.

> *Sidebar: Perhaps you've got one nightmare client who robs your time and energy and fills up your inbox with never-ending questions about how you prepare your salad dressing and whether you use locally harvested sea salt or not, and they only provide $71 a month. Guess what? That particular client needs to start behaving properly, or pay more, or you need to fire them and bid them farewell. Because right now, they're waaaaay below your ideal monthly client value, and they're making it damn near impossible to have your dream schedule. They're clogging up too much time and not providing anywhere near enough to make it "worth it" for you. Put bluntly: You cannot "afford" to keep working with this client. You can see by calculating your ideal monthly client value that it makes it a lot easier to determine which clients are the right fit and which are not.*

You just calculated your *ideal* monthly client value.

But what is your *current* monthly client value—right now? Let me show you how to find out.

Add up all sales from the last full month.

For instance, if this is June 16th, add up total sales for the entire month of May.

Divide that number by the total number of clients you served in the last full month.

If last month you made $7,500 selling your meal plans and you delivered meals to 20 clients, then your current monthly client value is $375.

$7,500 / 20 = $375

Last month, each client provided $375 to your business, on average. That's your *current monthly client value*. To phrase that differently, each client is currently "worth" $375 to your business.

This means that, based on the $500 ideal monthly client value you NEED to reach your monthly revenue with 30% profit, you're undercharging each client by $125 per month. Yikes!

Yikes…but also yay! Because now the solution is becoming apparent. You don't necessarily need more clients. You need the same number of clients (or fewer, potentially!) and different pricing. For instance, if you retain those 20 clients who adore you and increase each person's monthly invoice by $125, boom-shaka-laka! Just like that, you shifted your business from "struggling" to "healthy and sustainable, with a nice profit baked in."

EXAMPLE: MASSAGE THERAPIST

Another example for you. Let's pretend you're a massage therapist—like the example I referenced in the previous chapter. Currently, you conduct 90 massages per month on 60 clients. You're currently generating $9,000 per month, which means your current monthly client value is $150.

$9,000 / 60 = \$150$

$150 is your current monthly client value. In other words, currently, each client provides $150 per month (on average) to your business.

> *Does it feel like you're reading a word problem from your third-grade math class? "If train A leaves the station going 60 miles per hour and train B leaves one hour later going 85 miles per hour, how long will it take train B to catch up with train A?" Stick with me, and I'll have you arriving at your station very shortly! Choo choooo!*

Back to the massage example. You're currently conducting 90 massages a month on 60 clients. In the previous chapter, however, you determined that—in your dream schedule—you only have the capacity for 40 clients per month. And you did the math to calculate that your monthly revenue needed with 30% profit is $12,000 per month. How much should those 40 clients be paying each month?

$12,000 / 40 = \$300$

Aha! So your ideal monthly client value is $300. Going forward, each client should be paying you $300 per month, not $150! You're charging HALF what you should be charging and working more hours than you want to be working. No wonder you feel overworked and underpaid because you ARE!

> *A note on tips. You could say to your clients, "It's $300 per massage, and there's no need to add a tip. That's the full price. We've included gratuity in our prices." This makes things easier for you (as the business owner) and cleaner and easier for the client too.*

1. Calculate your ideal monthly client value.

Remember, the formula is very simple.

Monthly revenue needed with 30% profit baked in / ideal monthly client capacity = your ideal monthly client value

For instance, $10,000 per month (what you need to earn) / 20 clients (number of clients you can comfortably serve) = $500 per client.

Based on your dream schedule, you have the capacity to serve 20 clients per month. Each client must pay you an average of $500 per month for you to hit your monthly revenue goal and have your dream schedule.

$500 per client per month is what you need to run a healthy, profit-generating business. This is what the math says. It is non-negotiable. It is what it is.

Do the math to find your own numbers.

Monthly revenue needed with 30% profit   _____

/

Ideal monthly client capacity   _____

=

Ideal monthly client value   _____

2. Calculate your current monthly client value.

Current monthly revenue (last full month) / current active clients = current monthly client value

Current monthly revenue _____

/

Current active clients _____

=

Current monthly client value _____

Let's say you earned $7,500 last month and served 20 clients. $7,500 divided by 20 is $375. So your current monthly client value is $375. But what you need is $500. This means there's a gap of $125 between where you are—and where you need to be. How do you bridge this gap? There are different ways to do this.

One option is to keep your business exactly as it is—same menu, same services—nothing changes, except that you raise your prices. Same biz. New prices. Simple. This is absolutely an option. Businesses do this all the time. The price of gas goes up. The price of rent goes up. All kinds of things go up periodically—and your services can too.

However, another option is that you roll out a new menu of services! You can notify your current (and future) clients about your new, exciting, premium offers. New things you haven't offered before! This could be a new package, bundle, program, or something else that makes your clients go, "Ooh! That sounds amazing! Gimme that!"

For instance, you could roll out a VIP massage club membership that includes two massages per month, a custom aromatherapy oil blend, and a collection of guided audio recordings clients can play to meditate at home. It's so much more than just a massage or two. It's a powerful wellness experience, and you can charge accordingly. That's just one quick example of how rolling out a new offer could look. I have many more ideas to share with you.

In the next chapter (quite possibly my favorite in the entire book!), we're going to create pricing and packages that get you from wherever you are now to where you ultimately want to be.

CHAPTER 15:
Create Recurring Pricing

In the last chapter, you figured out your ideal monthly client value. This is the amount each client needs to provide to your business each month, on average.

Maybe you discovered that your ideal monthly client value is $500 or $1,750 or $4,444 or something else! Going forward, this is what each client needs to pay each month for you to have your dream schedule and hit your monthly revenue needs.

WHAT ARE YOU CHOOSING?

Earlier in this book, I mentioned that you are perfectly entitled to undercut your pricing. This feels like a good moment to reiterate this point.

You want to charge less? Sure, that's your prerogative as a business owner.

If you give a couple of clients a special "friend discount" so that they're only paying $225 a month instead of the $500 you need, that's a choice you can make.

But what are you choosing, really? You are choosing to work extra hours each week to catch up financially and hit your monthly revenue needs. You are choosing to add more stress to your life. You are choosing to spend less time with your family. Always remember this. You can choose to charge less than your ideal monthly client value, but in doing so, you're choosing a life you don't want.

Let's pause for a long, somber moment to let that sink in!

Okay, my friend. Now that I've shaken some sense into you, this chapter is all about how to create...recurring pricing. Ahhh. *Recurring* and *pricing*. These are two of my favorite words—especially when combined like a freshly baked baguette and Brie cheese!

NON-RECURRING VS. RECURRING PRICING

In this chappy (that's my new slang for chapter, do you like it?), I will show you how to create new pricing that guarantees you will reach your monthly revenue needs—every month. This isn't going to happen, though, with non-recurring pricing options. For a healthy, sustainable business, you want to create recurring pricing options.

"What's the difference?" you ask.

Non-recurring pricing means one-time payments that may (or may not) happen again.

For example, you charge a flat rate per massage when a client gets a massage or you sell a package of five massages that the client can use anytime in the next year. "When" is the key word here because there is no guarantee when your client will redeem all of their massages. With one-time payments, your business won't collect another payment—and receive more cash—until your client redeems all of their prepaid sessions. Or, in the case of the single massage purchase, there is no guarantee that your client will ever return to your business for another massage, let alone when that might occur! It's all very unpredictable.

This is a recipe for inconsistent monthly income. One month you generate $10,000 in revenue because you sold several five packs of massages. But the next month, you only generate $3,000 in revenue because none of your clients needed to purchase additional massages. Instead, you're waiting for your clients to use up their prepaid massages this month. It's a feast-or-famine cycle, and it's incredibly stressful.

What makes this extra frustrating is that you never know when those clients will redeem all of their massages. It could take them months—especially if, on average, your clients only schedule massages 1.5 times per month (throwback to Chapter 13, where I showed you how to calculate your monthly client utilization!).

Five massages purchased / 1.5 monthly client usage = 3.33 months (with the vinculum, the little horizontal line, over the repeating decimals. Total math nerd vocabulary. Feel free to roll your eyes and tell me to chill out on the math linguistics.)

"Jeez," you think. "At this rate, my clients won't pay me again for at least another three and a half months! How am I going to get cash this month?"

THE NON-RECURRING NIGHTMARE

To keep cash flowing and keep your business afloat, you find yourself forced to chase after new clients and convince people to buy more packages. This is a vicious cycle.

Like a drug, the feel-good high that comes from an immediate cash injection—achieved when you sell a few five packs of massages—quickly wears off the following month when you're just sitting on prepaid packages waiting for them to be redeemed and serviced.

Or, even worse, you become desperate for new clients to come in the door, so you focus intensely on marketing, advertising, and lead generation, trying as hard as you can to bring a new cash infusion into your business.

You're so busy trying to hustle and get new clients that you're spending all your attention there. Meanwhile, your current clients are getting neglected and not getting your best work. You're showing up to sessions bedraggled and distracted because you are overextended from trying to woo new clients! It becomes difficult to retain your current clients when you're offering a worn-out, half-assed version of yourself.

Can you see how non-recurring pricing leads to unpredictable income, weary business owners, and grumpy clients too? Lose-lose for everyone.

I found myself in this miserable trap during the first five years of owning my Pilates studio. Do you want to hear the tragic story? Of course you do! Grab your popcorn!

MY SUMMER OF DOOM AND DESPAIR

Like every other Pilates studio in my area, I sold private sessions and 10 and 20 packs of classes. The larger the pack, the less I charged per class.

I sold a ton of these 10 and 20 packs during the winter season when snowbirds from colder climates flocked to South Florida to escape the snow and settle into their winter homes for five to six months. From October to March, which locals simply call "season," my studio was slamming. But during the summer months, when the snowbirds were gone and back at their homes up north, none of their sessions were being redeemed, very few people were buying new class packs, and very little cash was coming in. My business was sitting on unused prepaid packages for half of the year, which meant no cash from these clients for half of the year.

I panicked and decided to do something BIG to drum up sales. I threw together my studio's first-ever Christmas in July sale.

My plan: "I'm going to offer 10% off all of my 10 and 20 class packs. And I'm going to let all of my clients buy as many packages as they want, even my snowbird clients who aren't here right now."

Mass emails were sent. Individual clients were called. Announcements were made daily in-studio. Sales were coming in left and right. Clients were purchasing multiple 10 and 20 packs each.

I thought I was a genius! Look at all this money pouring in! My master plan was working!

Well, a genius I was not! Sure, that month I generated over $20,000 in revenue from the "Christmas in July" sale. My business had never made that much money at one time before. I was elated. "I'm making it rain money!"

But do you want to know what happened the following month?

My studio made less than $3,000 in revenue.

Why? Because all of my clients purchased boatloads of sessions during the sale—at a discounted rate, mind you—which meant none of them needed to purchase sessions again for months and months. In fact, it took almost six months before my monthly revenue returned to normal levels—slowly increasing to $4,500, then $8,000, then just shy of $10,000, eventually making its way back up to the surface.

> *Lovely little detail: This Nightmare Before Christmas in July sale (see what I did there?) happened the same month I was recovering from viral meningitis. Talk about a compounding headache.*

After this debacle, I realized the error of my ways:

"I've been doing non-recurring pricing, where clients buy something once and then never purchase again—or don't purchase again for a very long time."

"What I need to do…is switch to a recurring pricing model."

RECURRING PRICING

Today, I am basically an evangelist for recurring pricing. I talk about it constantly. I urge all of my clients to do this. If I could sneak into every business-woman's bedroom and whisper "recurrrrring" into her ears as she's drifting to sleep (like a Pricing Tooth Fairy!), I would! And no, this is NOT creepy at all!

Recurring pricing is a much more sustainable business model because it guarantees payments every single month. Instead of collecting large payments at one time and waiting for services to be redeemed, your clients pay you the same amount each month automatically. Doesn't that just make your shoulders drop with relief? Guaranteed. Money. Every. Month. So soothing.

Not only does this allow you to predict your business income accurately, but clients love it too, because they are never hit with a large bill upfront or a massive invoice unexpectedly. It allows them to spread out their payments in smaller, more digestible chunks. It's a win-win for everyone involved.

Of course, if a client wishes to pay in full for her services, more power to her—and you. For instance, if a client wants to pay for a 12-month membership upfront rather than monthly chunks, great! You can happily accept PIFs (pay in fulls) without your entire business model being dependent on them.

RECURRING PRICING: EXAMPLES

So what does shifting to a recurring pricing model look like?

In the following examples, each business offers its own unique pricing, but they all build their pricing options around two factors: monthly client value and monthly client utilization.

BOUTIQUE FITNESS STUDIOS, GYMS, PERSONAL TRAINERS, YOGA INSTRUCTORS (AND SIMILAR BUSINESSES)

I'll start by using my Pilates studio as an example.

Once I switched to a recurring pricing model, it looked like this:

As a client, you can choose between four classes a month, eight classes a month, or unlimited classes a month.

Once you choose your frequency of classes, next you choose how long you want to commit to taking classes at the studio: month-to-month, six months, or 12 months.

You're willing to commit to more classes and a longer frequency? Sweet!

You get a slight price reduction. Simply put, the more classes you agree to take (monthly client utilization) and the longer you agree to do so (length of membership), the less you're going to pay.

It looked something like this.

> 4 classes a month on a month-to-month basis = $170 per month
> 4 classes a month for 6 months = $150 per month
> 4 classes a month for 12 months = $130 per month

When given these options, the majority of my clients—with the exception of my snowbird clients, the folks only visiting town for the winter months—chose the 12-month option because the monthly payment was the lowest. Who doesn't want to pay less?

By doing so, my business locked in a guaranteed payment of $130 per month for an entire year! Hello, predictable income AND long-term client!

Even my snowbird clients had an opportunity to save money when they chose the six-month option over the month-to-month option. In fact, several chose to spread out their six-month memberships into 12 monthly payments so that they paid less each month. I encouraged it because this meant that the studio was still receiving a payment from them even when they were up north for six months. Hello, stable cash flow! Where have you been all my life?!

"But what about the monthly client value?" asks no one! But I will explain nonetheless.

Let's circle back to that ideal monthly client value. We didn't do all of that math just to throw it away and not use it! Whatever your ideal monthly client value is, that's what you will charge for your mid-tier package, because the mid-tier package is what the majority of your clients will select.

Sticking with my Pilates studio as an example, let's pretend that my monthly client utilization was eight classes per month (meaning, the majority of my clients take eight classes per month) and my ideal monthly client value was $250 (meaning, this is how much each client needs to provide to my business per month for me to hit my revenue goals).

Holding this in mind, I want to price my mid-tier option at—or above—$250.

> 8 classes a month on a month-to-month basis = $270 per month
> 8 classes a month for 6 months = $250 per month
> 8 classes a month for 12 months = $230 per month

You'll notice that the average between all three monthly payment options is $250, which keeps my studio right on target to hit its ideal monthly client value.

See how this works?

My Pilates studio also offered unlimited class options to take this one step further. So, continuing with the same pattern, the pricing looked something like this.

> Unlimited classes a month on a month-to-month basis = $370 per month
> Unlimited classes a month for 6 months = $350 per month
> Unlimited classes a month for 12 months = $330 per month

While these weren't the exact prices at my studio (I honestly couldn't tell you what the actual prices were because this was maaaaa-aaany years ago), this gives you a solid idea of how I built my prices.

When laid out all together inside a pretty pricing booklet, you can see how my ideal monthly client value of $250 was the average monthly price across all pricing options offered at my studio.

> 4 classes a month on a month-to-month basis = $170 per month
> 4 classes a month for 6 months = $150 per month
> 4 classes a month for 12 months = $130 per month
>
> 8 classes a month on a month-to-month basis = $270 per month
> 8 classes a month for 6 months = $250 per month
> 8 classes a month for 12 months = $230 per month
>
> Unlimited classes a month on a month-to-month basis =
> $370 per month
> Unlimited classes a month for 6 months = $350 per month
> Unlimited classes a month for 12 months = $330 per month

The majority of my clients purchased the mid-tier membership of eight classes per month. And it was an absolute pleasure to get clients signed up for recurring packages so that I could charge their credit card once a month, after month, after month…ongoing. Stable revenue for my business. Small monthly payments for my clients.

Plus, getting that monthly charge provided motivation for each client to get their ass into the studio to take classes, and meant certain clients became even more consistent with their workouts. A total win-win for everyone involved! And no more meningitis hospital visits for yours truly!

SPA, SALON, AND WELLNESS SERVICES: MASSAGE, FACIALS, BODYWORK, REIKI, ACUPUNCTURE

Let's role-play and pretend you're a massage therapist. As you may recall from previous chapters, we determined that your ideal monthly client value needs to be $300 per month, and your monthly client utilization is 1.5 massages per month.

Of course, you aren't going to offer a package that gives your clients 1.5 massages per month because that would be…weird. But you could create a package that gives your clients one 90-minute massage per month!

When we calculated the monthly client utilization for this example, we calculated based on the hour: 60 minutes. If you multiply your 1.5 monthly client utilization by 60 minutes, you get 90 minutes, so wouldn't it make sense to now offer a pricing option that gives your clients one 90-minute massage for $300 per month?

It could look something like this.

One 90-minute massage per month on a month-to-month basis = $325 per month

One 90-minute massage per month for 6 months = $300 per month

One 90-minute massage per month for 12 months = $275 per month

---

Again, the monthly client utilization of 1.5 massages per month—which we converted into one 90-minute massage—and your monthly client value of $300 are the components of your mid-tier pricing option. Boom!

Now, instead of your clients coming inconsistently for 60-minute massages—averaging only 1.5 times per month—you have now streamlined your schedule and transitioned your clients to longer massages more consistently.

Can you see how this not only benefits your schedule and your business revenue, but it also benefits your clients? When your clients get a 90-minute massage every single month, they have less pain, sleep better at night, and have less stress overall. I'll say it again: win *fucking* win!

Sticking with this same example, let's pretend you are a massage therapist who ONLY wants to conduct 60-minute massages. Ninety minutes is too long for you. So, instead of converting your monthly client utilization of 1.5 massages per month into one 90-minute massage per month, you're going to offer a pricing option that gives your clients two 60-minute massages per month. By doing so, your monthly client utilization will inevitably increase from 1.5 to 2!

But how do you determine the price point for two massages per month? Simple!

You take your ideal monthly client value of $300 and divide it by your monthly client utilization of 1.5 to get $200 per massage.

$300 ideal monthly client value / 1.5 monthly client utilization = $200 per massage

This means that your pricing option for two massages per month needs to cost $400 per month.

$200 per massage x 2 per month = $400 per month

It could look something like this.

One 60-minute massage per month = $225 per month

Two 60-minute massages per month = $400 per month (Remember: You want your mid-tier option to be your ideal monthly client value—stick it right in the middle. "That's what she said." I'm sorry, but this joke never gets old!)

Four 60-minute massages per month = $700 per month (One massage per week? Sign me up!)

"Erin, how did you get the prices for the other two options?" you might be questioning.

I'm happy to explain.

If two massages per month equals $400 per month, then that means each massage is $200, but just like in the example I gave of my Pilates studio, you want to incentivize your clients with discounts on services when they commit to using your services more frequently—thereby increasing their client utilization.

If a client only commits to one massage per month, she will pay more than $200 per massage. That's where I settled on $225 per massage.

If a client commits to more massages, like four massages a month, she will pay less than $200 per massage. That's where I settled on $175 per massage.

When you look at the pricing options again, this time look at the per massage rate.

One 60-minute massage per month = $225 per month
($225 per month / 1 massage = $225 per massage)

Two 60-minute massages per month = $400 per month
($400 per month / 2 massages = $200 per massage)

Four 60-minute massages per month = $700 per month
($700 per month / 4 massages = $175 per massage)

This is the perfect example of how you can incentivize your clients with discounts when they increase their client utilization.

Do you HAVE to offer a price reduction for clients who purchase a higher quantity? Nope! It's a common practice but not required. Certain brands—think an extremely high-end luxury brand like Tiffany jewelry—probably aren't going to make a price reduction even if you're buying three diamond bracelets every month. The price is what it is, no matter how much you buy. However, many businesses offer a lower-price incentive for clients who utilize services more often. It can be a smart move.

ONLINE SERVICES: VIRTUAL ASSISTANTS, COPYWRITERS, WEB DEVELOPERS, BOOKKEEPERS, ETC.

I want to give you another example. This time, you're going to step into the world of online services.

Imagine that you are a virtual assistant and you calculated that your ideal monthly client value needs to be $1,500, and your monthly client utilization is 40 hours per month. You only work with clients on a month-to-month basis—no long-term contracts here—so you will start by pricing your most utilized package, 40 hours per month, at $1,500.

Up to 40 hours per month = $1,500 per month

Notice how I named this pricing option "up to 40 hours per month?"

With online services such as these, your services can be variable. Some months, your clients may only need 34 hours, but other months, they may need all 40. To get yourself off the clock-in/clock-out bill cycle, build pricing options that give your clients "up to" a certain number of hours per month.

This is called a *monthly retainer*. Your client pays for up to 40 hours per month, and they need to use those 40 hours in one month. Use it or lose it. Essentially, you are saying to the client, "I am going to set aside 40 hours for you this month. That time is all yours. But it's up to you to assign me 40 hours worth of work."

The client pays for 40 hours even if they don't have exactly 40 hours of work for you to do, which means that you get paid the same amount each month regardless of whether the client uses up exactly 40 hours or 35 or 29.5 or whatever amount, which means more stability for you.

So let's say you set your average pricing option: up to 40 hours per month for $1,500 per month.

Then, you will build other pricing tiers around your most utilized pricing option—one smaller (20 hours per month) and one larger (60 hours per month)—so that you set yourself up to reach your ideal monthly client value on average across all pricing options you offer.

Up to 20 hours per month = $800 per month

Up to 40 hours per month = $1,500 per month

Up to 60 hours per month = $2,100 per month

As you can see, you're incentivizing clients who use more of your services with a lower price for those services.

Using the pricing options above for your virtual assistant business, let's break down the hourly rate your clients will pay.

Up to 20 hours per month = $800 per month
($800 per month / 20 hours = $40 per hour)

Up to 40 hours per month = $1,500 per month
($1,500 per month / 40 hours = $37.50 per hour)

Up to 60 hours per month = $2,100 per month
($2,100 per month / 60 hours = $35 per hour)

The more hours your clients commit to, the less your clients pay per hour. But don't get too caught up in the per-hour rate game because remember—your client may or may not use all of the hours available to them each month. How much you charge per hour is less important than the amount you charge per month. And you always want to charge a monthly rate equivalent to your ideal monthly client value. Deal?

Do you feel as though you're catching on but could use a few more examples?

"Yes, ma'am."

Okay. Here come two more.

PROGRAMMED SERVICES: NUTRITIONISTS, PHYSICAL THERAPISTS, CHIROPRACTORS, ETC.

I have worked with many practitioners who own programmed services, meaning they offer a specific program that clients enter into for a certain period of time. The client eventually graduates from that program into a different service option. A great example of this type of business is a chiropractor.

Back to role-playing, we go. This time, you are a chiropractor who owns a cash practice, meaning you don't bill insurance.

You have two types of clients: new clients who come to you for the first time in acute pain after an injury or accident, and repeat clients who are no longer in acute pain but come to you for maintenance.

The new clients typically come in 12 times a month. The repeat clients, only two times.

Since both types of clients differ so vastly in how frequently they use your services, you decide to calculate the monthly client utilization separately for both types of clients.

Your business has the capacity for 100 clients per month: 25 new clients whose monthly client utilization is 12 visits per month and 75 repeat clients whose monthly utilization is two visits per month.

The typical new client seeks your services after an injury and utilizes your services intensely for three months before graduating into a maintenance program. Although you calculated that the monthly client utilization for new clients is 12 visits per month, you also know that those visits consist of several different services that you offer at your practice, depending on what the client needs on any given day: x-rays, exams, adjustments, transcutaneous electrical nerve stimulation (tens unit), exercise machines, massage chair, heating pads, ice therapy, etc.

For ease of pricing, without having to charge your clients for each individual service they receive, you can offer a three-month *Get Out Of Pain* plan that all new clients begin with. And you can notify new clients, "We require that all new clients begin with this plan."

Then, your repeat clients are no longer in acute pain but continue using your services on an as-needed basis to maintain their overall wellness. Just like your new clients, they also like to use all of the services you offer, not just adjustments. Keep their pricing option simple and create one Maintenance plan they can use every single month, ongoing, for as long as they'd like.

You did all of the math up until this point, and you calculated that your monthly revenue needed with 30% profit baked in is $50,000. Half of your monthly revenue (50%) comes from new clients and the other half (50%) comes from repeat clients. How much should you charge for each plan?

"Erin, this word problem is looking more and more like that stupid train problem, and I think I am about to derail...I'm about to need a chiropractic adjustment right now because I am stiffening up! Too much math!!"

This might be a good time to tell the little conductor in your head to stay on the tracks because this math is so simple, it's going to blow your mind. You got this!

Let's first calculate the price for the new client *Get Out Of Pain* plan.

$50,000 monthly revenue needed x 50% = $25,000 monthly revenue needed from new clients

$25,000 monthly revenue needed / 25 clients = $1,000 monthly client value[2]

That's it! The price for your Get Out Of Pain plan is $1,000 per month for three months! Done.

Now, let's calculate the price for your repeat client *Maintenance* plan.

$50,000 monthly revenue needed x 50% = $25,000 monthly revenue needed from repeat clients

$25,000 monthly revenue needed / 75 clients = $333 monthly client value

So the price for your Maintenance plan is $333 per month.

You now offer TWO simple plans that your clients choose from and pay for automatically every month. Your business wins because you've secured guaranteed monthly revenue. Your clients win because they have regular access to your services for as long as they wish!

Do you have enough steam in your locomotive engine for one more example?

"I think I can. I think I can. I think I can," says the Little Engine That Could. (How obvious is it that I'm a mom of two?)

---

2   Remember, in this example, your business has the capacity for 100 clients per month: 25 new clients whose monthly client utilization is 12 visits per month and 75 repeat clients whose monthly utilization is two visits per month. That's why we're using 25 in this equation.

COACHES, CONSULTANTS, AND OTHER VALUE-BASED SERVICE PROVIDERS

What is *value-based pricing*? This means you set your pricing based on the value of your services—instead of basing your pricing on a time/cost analysis with a profit margin baked in.

For instance, imagine you're a world-famous astrologer who has authored numerous bestselling books about how the cosmos influences your life. You're the personal astrologer for A-list celebrities. You have your own TV show. You are considered the best astro-guide in the industry. People weep during your sessions, find their purpose, and their lives are forever changed. To book a session with you? It might cost 20x more than most astrologers in the world, and that is A-OK! You can command this ultra-high pricing because you're a proven rockstar in your field. Clients will pay anything you request because getting one-on-one time with you is extremely valuable.

Another example: Let's say you're a publicist known as "the Oprah whisperer." You've helped more than 100 clients get featured in *O: The Oprah Magazine* and on *Good Morning America* and many other top outlets. You charge $20,000 daily for an all-day VIP experience where you help clients map out their PR strategy for the year. If you spend six hours jamming with the client during that all-day intensive, this hourly rate is $3,333. Ludicrous? Hell no! Because you have a stellar track record of success. You can confidently guarantee, "Hire me, and you will get major press coverage that brings $100,000 in revenue to your business—at minimum." Clients joyfully pay $20K per day because they know it will provide a huge ROI! See, clients aren't really paying you by the hour (they couldn't care less about the hourly rate). They're paying you based on the *value* you provide.

Those are two examples of value-based pricing.

"Erin, are you about to tell me to throw everything I just learned in this book out the window?"

Nope. Not even a chance. Stick with me.

While value-based pricing does not *depend* on the actual costs associated with running your business, you certainly want to make sure you're still reaching your monthly revenue needs so that you can cover your expenses, pay yourself, and make a profit! Your prices can go as high as you want—based on the value you provide.

How much value do you provide? The proof is in your clients' success stories, which can't be reduced to a price tag. What's important to remember is you *never* want your pricing options to fall below your ideal monthly client value.

Let's imagine that you're a coach—such as a life coach, wellness coach, relationship coach, or maybe a business coach. Coaching is a profession where many providers do value-based pricing. When coaches begin working with me to build out pricing options for their businesses, the most common first goal is hitting $10,000 per month in revenue. Ahh, the elusive $10K month! A big milestone for any new coach.

Here's the thing about running a coaching practice. Typically, your operating expenses are very low—much lower than running a brick-and-mortar business. As a coach, you need a laptop, WiFi, email account, Zoom, and a phone, and you're pretty much good to go! You're probably not renting an expensive studio or purchasing tons of pricey gym equipment. It's a very low-overhead profession.

To use myself as an example, when I first started coaching, my initial goal was to generate $10,000 per month in revenue. However, my monthly revenue needs were only $8,500—and that was after I paid myself $5,000 per month and baked in a 30% profit margin.

Then, I determined that my capacity for clients—based on my dream schedule—was 10 clients per month. And I divided $10,000 per month by 10 clients to give me an ideal monthly client value of $1,000 per client. So, when I first started coaching, my pricing was $1,000 per month per client.

What did my clients receive for $1,000 per month? They received two monthly calls, email support, membership to my private Facebook group, all of my pricing spreadsheets and templates, and access to my online courses.

Once $10,000 per month became the norm and demand for my services increased, so did my prices. With each increase, though, I maintained a client capacity of 10 clients per month.

When I increased my monthly goal from $10,000 to $15,000, my prices increased from $1,000 to $1,500 per month.

When I increased my monthly goal from $15,000 to $20,000, my prices increased from $1,500 to $2,000 per month.

By doing this, I was able to maintain my dream schedule, work with 10 clients a month (comfortable: not too many, just right), and increase my earnings significantly. As I became even more experienced and skilled at coaching—and as those client success stories piled up—I was able to command a higher price. Because I knew, "If you hire me, I can provide immense value to you. I can guarantee results."

At the time I'm writing this book, my standard coaching option is $5,555 per month, with different pricing options with different levels of access to me ranging from $1,111 per month upwards of $7,777 per month.

Each time I want to reach a new monthly revenue goal, I do the math and raise my prices to match my new ideal monthly client value.

To revisit that equation:

Monthly revenue needs (amount of money you need to earn) / ideal client capacity (number of clients you can comfortably serve) = ideal monthly client value (amount each client must pay)

ADDING MASSIVE VALUE TO YOUR SERVICES

Clients often say, "Erin, how am I supposed to charge $300 per massage? That's ludicrous!" Or, "$3,333 a month for nutrition and wellness coaching? Those prices will stupefy my clients. They'll think I have lost my damn mind!"

You might think, "When my clients see this new menu of services and new pricing, they're going to faint because it's so much higher than what they're accustomed to paying."

Here's the solution: *Add more value.*

Add massive value to your services, so the price feels worth it. Not just worth it, but actually a hot deal!

For instance, $300 for one massage might seem like a lot.

But it's so much more than just a massage. What if, for an ongoing payment of $300 per month, you receive:

- A glorious 90-minute massage (gratuity included)
- All the hot stone, hand and foot treatments, deep tissue, and scalp massage add-ons (without extra charge)
- A soothing waiting-room experience with organic tea, local honey, and aromatherapy air diffuser
- A custom massage oil-blend made especially for you
- Hot towels wrapped around your neck and feet
- Priority scheduling (you get first dibs on selecting your appointment date/time each month)
- A collection of ten audio meditations (pre-recorded) that you can listen to anytime when you need to de-stress and unwind

Okay, wowza! Now, suddenly, $300 sounds like an absolute deal! Because it's not $300 for one massage. It's $300 for an entire wellness experience.

As a business owner, this is the question you need to ask yourself, "How can I create massive value for my client—in a way that's really quick, easy, and free (or almost free) for me to deliver?"

I've got more ideas for you.

If you're a writer, you can provide writing services to your client and a collection of pre-written email, newsletter, and website templates they can use anytime. (You only need to create these templates once! And then give them to every new client who signs up to work with you. Massive value for your client. Zero extra work for you.)

If you run a chiropractic clinic, you can provide chiro services to your client—plus, clients who do your monthly recurring plan also get a collection of training videos to do at home, an anti-inflammatory meal plan, a list of recommended dietary supplements, and they're entered into a monthly drawing for a prize too. (Again, you only need to create the training videos and meal plan once. It could be really simple, like five short videos and a three-page PDF that outlines the plan. Easy for you to whip together. But it provides major value to your client.)

More ideas on how to add more value:

- Worksheets, checklists, templates (create it once, share it with an unlimited number of clients)
- Pre-recorded videos and audio (ditto, create it once, share it repeatedly)
- Monthly drawing to win a prize (pick a new client every month!)
- Monthly social hour where clients can meet other clients for a group workout, walk, or brunch
- Monthly Ask-Me-Anything hour when clients can write (or call in) to get answers to their burning questions (it only takes one hour of your time each month but provides major value to clients)
- Luxurious touches, like aromatherapy, cucumber water, and heated towels (things that don't cost much to provide: low cost, big impact)
- Personalized touches, like writing a client's pet's name on a chalkboard ("Welcome, Peanut!")—a magical moment whenever they drop off their pet at doggy daycare
- Upgraded environment, like a clinic, studio, or waiting room that's so beautiful people never want to leave
- Childcare on-site so the kids can play in a supervised zone while the parents do their session
- Special perks like priority scheduling, a designated locker space, or something else that would be majorly valuable for your clients

What's something that would make your clients go, "Oooooh, that sounds like a dream come true?"

What could you add to elevate your services from "ordinary" to "an unforgettable experience?"

Brainstorm how you could add massive value so that your new/higher pricing feels like the deal of the century.

Goal: You want your clients to think, "Wait, I get ALL THAT for [amount] per month? OMG. Are you serious? Sign me up!"

ONE-TIME SERVICES (AKA NON-RECURRING OPTIONS)

As you've learned in this chapter, I am the Queen of Recurring Revenue. I urge every business owner to figure out a recurring pricing model so that your clients pay you consistently every month. This model is a game-changer.

However, you may be thinking, "But, Erin, my particular business just doesn't work like that!"

You may argue and say, "I offer web design services. Clients hire me when they need a one-time website makeover. It's a one-time thing, not a recurring dealio."

Or you say, "I'm a wedding planner! People hire me once—at least, hopefully just once! It's one and done. They never hire me again."

I hear you. Nonetheless, I still insist that you can create recurring pricing. No matter what kind of profession you have, it's still possible to create a recurring model and get money flowing in repeatedly every month.

Here's how this might look.

WEB DESIGN

Offer a website makeover package for $7,000 (one time) and then a website maintenance service for $250 a month (ongoing).

The maintenance plan covers whenever your client wants to do little tweaks and updates (which she most assuredly will!). Boom. Recurring pricing is yours!

WEDDING PLANNER

Offer a deluxe, all-inclusive wedding planning service for $36,000 (one time), but let clients know that they can pay in monthly installments: $3,000 a month for 12 months (recurring). Now you've got predictable income, month after month.

Another option: Tell your client, "In addition to weddings, I love planning anniversary parties, baby showers, birthdays, and other special moments." You could offer a Honeymoon Forever package for $500 a month (ongoing), where you plan a mini celebration for the couple every month—a romantic picnic, a special date night, or something else that is incredibly special and memorable. The goal: Keep the honeymoon vibes flowing all year long! I mean, sign me up!

WRITER AND EDITOR

Let's say you're a writer and editor. Clients typically hire you to do a one-time project, like writing a big presentation or editing a book manuscript. You might sell your services by-the-package, such as "$10,000 to edit a manuscript."

But what if your client wants to purchase a few additional services in a month or two? They probably will! You know they're going to swing back into your inbox and say, "Oh, could you do this one other thing…." "Actually, I just thought of something else I need…."

For extra tweaks in the future, you can offer a weighted price (very high price, less appealing to your client) as well as a recurring price (much more reasonable price, more appealing).

For instance, say, "If you want to hire me for extra tasks in the future, here's how that works...."

One-time task: $250 an hour (this is your weighted price)

Monthly plan: $250 for three hours of writing/editing, whenever you need it, every month (this is your recurring price)

Why would anyone pay $250 per hour every time they need help when they can simply pay $250 per month and have triple the amount of support? No brainer!

WEIGHTED PRICING: MORE EXAMPLES

- $50 for one Pilates reformer class vs. $150 per month for four classes recurring
- $400 per massage vs. $300 per month for one massage recurring
- $1,888 per coaching call vs. $1,111 per month for one call per month + unlimited Voxer coaching recurring
- $500 per written piece vs. $1,500 per month for four pieces, daily social posts, and one email newsletter
- $150 per acupuncture treatment vs. $75 per month for one treatment recurring
- $750 for one graphic design vs. $750 per month for up to three graphics recurring

See how this works?

It's perfectly okay for some of your clients to pay as they go, but they need to pay a higher price when they do. By doing this, you make your one-time service less appealing and make your recurring service more appealing. The majority of your clients will opt for a recurring plan because...it's a no-brainer!

They get more bang for their buck, and you get the security and peace of mind that comes from recurring monthly revenue.

WHAT'S THE BEST RECURRING PRICING MODEL FOR YOU?

This chapter is all about…what? Recurring pricing!

Here's your homework assignment:

Start dreaming up a recurring pricing model for your business.

This could look like:

- Encouraging clients to purchase a membership (four, eight, or 12 classes a month with a recurring monthly charge)
- Getting your clients excited to buy a lengthier plan (six-month meal plan or a price reduction if they choose the 12-month plan)
- Asking clients to hire you on retainer (up to 20 hours a month, up to 40 hours a month, up to 60 hours a month, paid in full on the first of each month, with a minimum three-month time commitment)
- Offering a required three-month plan for new clients, followed by a maintenance plan for tune-ups
- Offering a menu with gratuity included so your client can pay one simple fee every month without needing to add tips into the equation

The goal is recurring revenue every month. Automatic monthly charge. More stability for you. More predictability, consistency, and better results for your clients. And, if you're offering a three-tiered pricing option, you want the mid-tier option to be your ideal monthly client value.

If you're thinking, "I just don't see how I can create a recurring pricing model for my particular business. I don't have any good ideas on how to do this!"… never fear, help is here. Go to www.pricingoverhaul.com, and you can hire me (or a Pricing Overhaul® Coach that I've personally trained and certified) to help you do this. You don't have to do this alone.

Recurring pricing is possible for every type of service-based business. My team and I have created recurring pricing for businesses you would otherwise think couldn't offer recurring pricing—including attorneys, accountants, hair stylists, photographers, makeup artists, distilleries (anyone interested in a vodka of the month club?), behavior analysts, dermatologists, and more.

Whatever service you offer, there is a recurring pricing model for you.

P.S. Scan the QR code at the end of this chapter to start building your new recurring pricing options. *Recurring* is about to become your all-time favorite word.

CHAPTER 16:
Roll Out Your New Pricing

You've done the math. You've figured out what you need to charge. You've chosen your new pricing. You've even figured out how to offer recurring services to your clients (hallelujah!), which means steady income every month, forever and ever.

You've got an excellent plan. Now it's time to roll it out!

Meaning that it's time to notify your current clients (and future clients) and let people know, "I've made some exciting changes. Here's what I'm offering now!"

What's the best way to do this? Should you simply update your website with your new pricing—and that's that? Or should you notify each client personally by sending an email? Call each client on the phone? Hold a town hall forum? Hire a pilot to write your new pricing in the sky with an airplane?! Or some other approach? What's the best way to roll things out and get people pumped about these changes?

That's exactly what we'll discuss in this chapter.

ALL THE FEELS

At this moment, you're probably feeling like:

"Erin, these new prices are just way too high. There is no way I can start charging this much."

"My clients are going to freak out. They'll leave and go find another cheaper service provider."

"My clients love me, but they just can't afford these new prices."

You might have a hundred different worries and hesitations tumbling around inside your head.

If that's you? Here's what I want you to do. Go back and read Part One of this book—again. That section is all about shifting your mindset. Flip through it again and get your mind back on track, because you need to be in the right headspace for your rollout plan to be successful.

If you believe "There is no way my clients will pay this much. I am going to lose all of my clients," guess what? Your clients *will not* pay the new rates and *will* leave.

As a business owner, the failure or success of your business starts with you. The way you think, the way you feel, the way you speak to yourself (and to clients), and how you carry yourself in the world. If you feel like an anxiety-riddled, insecure, self-doubting mess, then your business will be a hot mess (yes, that is the official terminology!) as well.

But, and this is a big but (cue: "Baby Got Back" by Sir Mix-a-Lot, my personal go-to power song!), if you go into your rollout *knowing* that your clients will pay the new prices because you are more than worth it, then your clients will stay with your business and pay the new prices—and they will do so happily.

Your attitude—and the attitude of your team—is the make-it-or-break-it factor in this process. It is THE sole thing that will determine how successful the rollout will be.

If you think it won't work, it won't work. If you think it will work, it will. Period. This is true with everything you do in life. So choose your thoughts carefully as you begin your rollout.

YOU ARE HITTING A NEW LEVEL

Not everyone will come along with you for the ride when you go through an uplevel. The people who are meant to rise with you will. The people who are not will not. Uplevel anyway.

Because you, my dear friend, are going through a major uplevel. Your uplevel began the moment you picked up this book. Your uplevel continued as you read each chapter and did the math. And your uplevel accelerates now as you roll out your new prices. Despite all the fear and doubt, uplevel anyway!

Accept the fact that not everyone is going to cheer for your uplevel. Most people will. A few will not. Even with the best attitude, best strategy, and best intentions, you might lose a few clients during the rollout. I want to remind you: This is OKAY.

You might lose a small handful of clients. And this will open up space for new dream clients to come work with you. Ultimately, it's not a loss. It's a win.

PLAN YOUR ROLLOUT

So what's the best way to roll out your new pricing—so that you feel confident, your team (if you have one) feels excited, and you retain as many clients as possible?

There is no "one way" you must roll out your new pricing. There are many options. In this chapter, I'm going to share a few strategies my clients have used—with great success.

Ultimately, you have to trust your instincts and go with the strategy that feels right to you. Your rollout plan must be in alignment with your values. As a business owner, what do you value most highly? Maybe it's kindness, simplicity, community, generosity, ease, beauty, justice, vitality, power, luxury, speed, or another quality. Whatever you value, create a rollout plan that expresses those values.

Do what feels right—and the majority of your clients will come along with you for the ride.

START WITH BRAND NEW CLIENTS

The best way to gain confidence in your new prices…is to roll out the new prices to *new clients* first.

Yes, I give you permission to keep your existing clients at their prices for a short time. You'll notify them about your new pricing very soon. But for now, get your feet wet, bringing new clients on board at your new rates.

Once you see that new clients are paying your new prices without hesitation, you'll feel even more confident about announcing your new pricing to current clients.

The beauty of new clients is that they are *new*. They don't know how you used to operate. They don't know how much you charged three weeks ago! All they know is that these are the prices now, plain and simple, meaning new clients are less likely to question your prices—forcing you to defend yourself and your new rates—since they don't know any difference.

When a new client trots into your business or emails you to inquire about working together, do *not* say:

"Great to meet you! I recently increased my prices, and here's the new menu and new pricing…."

No, no, no! Instead, say:

"I'd love to work with you! Here's my menu of services and pricing."

Your tone needs to convey, "This is what I offer, and this is how much it costs." Calm, cool, collected. Never mind the fact that you completely changed your pricing—12 hours ago. This new client doesn't need to know that—and it's not relevant! All they need to know is what you're offering right now.

GET YOUR TEAM ON BOARD

Before rolling out your new prices with new clients, get your staff fully on board.

Schedule a staff meeting to do sales training. Go through the pricing changes. Explain why you must make the changes. Answer any questions they've got. And explain why these changes are a *win-win-win* situation. You, your team, and the clients—everyone wins.

"What's in it for me?" is always on your staff's mind, so be sure to emphasize the benefits to them—more consistent schedules, higher paychecks (when the business makes more, they make more), and a happier work environment with more abundance and less stress. Not to mention that you'll all be providing a higher-quality experience to each client.

Even if you have certain team members who won't be responsible for selling services to clients, it's a good idea to make them aware of the new pricing. You want your entire team to be informed, on the same page, and unified around these changes.

Order food, feed your team, and make this staff meeting feel celebratory and fun. The vibe is "We're rising to a new level! We will become the premium provider in the region—the best in the industry!" This is an exciting moment for everyone on the team.

ROLE-PLAY WITH YOUR TEAM

When training your staff, do role-playing. Practice going through different scenarios, such as:

"Hi, I just moved to town, and I'd like to become a client. Can you walk me through the options?"

"Hey, I heard about you from a friend, and I'm interested in your [such-and-such] package. Do you still offer that?"

"I used to be a client—years ago. I'm back! I'd like to enroll again."

"Wow, this sounds amazing, but it's out of my budget."

"Oh, I'm just browsing right now. I don't need anything at the moment…."

Teach your team what to do—and say—in these scenarios. Rehearse together, just like you're actors preparing for your debut on *Saturday Night Live.* Have one team member play the "client" and another play the "salesperson." Rehearse each scenario at least three times. You want each team member to feel completely confident and unflappable.

What do clients and dogs have in common? They can smell fear. Okay, to be honest, I don't know if this is a scientific fact—but my dad used to say it to me all the time, so I'm sticking with it. If your staff feels nervous and unprepared, your clients will smell the fear—and walk right out the door.

That's why role-playing is essential. Keep practicing until each team member feels rock-solid about the new pricing—zero hesitation when quoting prices and asking for the sale.

UPDATE YOUR WEBSITE (AND OTHER MARKETING MATERIALS) WITH THE NEW PRICES

Most clients find your business online and scope out your website before they pick up the phone, email, or DM your business to get started.

The last thing you want is for a new client to see your old pricing on the website—only to be taken aback when you quote the new prices. That feels like a bait-and-switch. It's a bummer for everyone involved. The same goes for anywhere online where your prices may be listed: social media, Yelp, online marketplaces, and so on.

It's time to update, update, update across the board!

- Discard printed materials that display the old pricing (pricing sheets, signage, contracts, referral cards, postcards, etc.) and print new materials with the new pricing proudly displayed.

- Make sure you code your business POS (point of sale) system with the new prices.
- Make sure that all payment links (for online businesses) have either been deactivated (if they are at the old prices) or created (with the new prices) and replaced with the appropriate links. Because you don't want a new client to purchase your service online at the old price unknowingly—and then you're stuck serving that client at the old rate.
- Update all materials as best you can. If you miss something (oops) and a new client says, "Wait a sec, I thought the price was XYZ," respond by saying, "You're right! That used to be the price. But that's actually an old document that's out of date. We rolled out a completely new menu, and here's the new pricing. So sorry about the confusion." Apologize briefly and move on. Don't make it a bigger deal than it is.

NOTIFY EXISTING CLIENTS

You've been selling your new pricing to new clients for one month or so. You're feeling more confident about the new pricing. Now it's time to notify your existing clients. For many business owners, this is the scariest moment. Getting heart palpitations? Where did you place your glass of wine? Take a sip and continue reading.

Who should notify existing clients? A member of your team? You personally?

I recommend that you, the owner, be the one to notify your existing clients about pricing changes.

Or, if you own a larger company and clients are used to interacting with a manager instead of you, this person can notify existing clients. But for most small businesses, the person delivering the message should be you.

You want this message to come from someone within your company who is an authority figure. In other words, you don't want your part-time receptionist or brand-new intern to be the person responsible for notifying clients about the new pricing. Because you don't want grumpy clients saying, "I want to speak to a manager," and then disrespecting and steamrolling right over this poor staff member who is just trying their best!

Unfortunately, I've seen this happen. One time, this exact scenario played out for a client of mine. Names have been changed to protect the innocent. Cue the theme song for *Law & Order*. Let's call her "Vicky."

Vicky was so nervous about notifying existing clients about the price increase. Rather than do it herself, she passed this task off to a part-time front desk staff member. Let's call her "Lisa."

Several weeks later, Vicky and I hopped on the phone to do a follow-up call. She was miserable because none of her existing clients had transitioned over to the new pricing. In fact, disgruntled clients flooded the company inbox and voicemail with complaints. Yikes.

"When clients call you to complain, what are they saying?" I asked, hoping to get to the bottom of this dilemma.

"Well, they're not calling me," she confessed. "They're speaking to Lisa."

"Who is Lisa?" I wondered. I'd never heard Lisa's name come up during our coaching calls together. Did Vicky have an imaginary friend I didn't know about?!

"Lisa is someone I hired recently," Vicky explained timidly. "She works the front desk part-time now."

Code red! Immediately, the problem was crystal clear. Vicky was anxious about notifying her clients. As a result, her staff felt insecure and wasn't fully on board either. Worst of all, Vicky pawned an important task onto a brand-new staff member—the aforementioned Lisa—who never received the proper sales training to do this task successfully. Big yikes across the board. No wonder this plan didn't go very well!

Vicky's clients could immediately smell Lisa's fear, and Lisa's uncertainty made the clients feel equally uncertain too. Now Vicky has to speak with each client individually to address their concerns and put out fires.

If Vicky had simply notified the clients personally, she could have avoided this whole drama.

"Okay, Vicky," I replied. "We need to do some role-playing."

Together, we practiced how Vicky would personally call each client, what to say, and how to convey a clear, confident tone. I am happy to report that Vicky successfully transitioned the remaining clients with ease. Phew. Crisis averted!

Which leads to my next topic. What is the best method of notification? Email, phone, Zoom, in-person?

The answer depends on you and your business. How do you normally communicate with your clients?

If you normally communicate with them in-person, then speaking face-to-face is best.

If you normally communicate with your clients via Zoom, speak with the client about the changes via Zoom.

If you mainly communicate with your clients via email, send an email to the client notifying them about the changes.

There is no one right method of communication, but there is one wrong method, and that is via mass communication.

MASS COMMUNICATION = MASS CHAOS

Mass communication looks like a generic social media post, a mass text, a mass email, or a recorded voice memo that gets sent to all of your clients' phones.

You know that horror movie music? *Reee reee reeeee!* Terrible high-pitched screeching sounds while the unsuspecting protagonist lathers up in the shower? That's what I hear inside my head when a client says, "Oh, I'm just going to blast out an email to my entire contact list." Nooooo!

When you send out a generic mass communication, it tends to create pandemonium.

Clients gossip amongst one another. "Did you see the email Erin just sent? Can you believe how much the prices are going up?"

Clients feel disrespected. "This is so impersonal. I've been a client for five years! Don't I at least deserve a personal email or call about this?"

Clients feel confused and bubble over with a million questions. "Wait, does this new pricing apply to me? Or just new clients? When does it go into effect? What about the services I already purchased—are those still valid? I got a gift certificate last week—will the old pricing be honored for that? And what about...."

Cue your phone ringing off the hook, your inbox flooding with emails, notifications dinging like crazy from social media comments. Aaaaahhhhhh!!!!!! Where's the fire extinguisher?

No mass communication. Please. Not for your existing clients. Even though it takes more effort, reach out to existing clients personally, one by one, to notify them about the new pricing.

Explain the new pricing. Explain why this is an exciting moment—your business is getting an upgrade, premium services, an even better experience for each client, win-win for everyone. Give them a moment to digest the info.

Then ask, "Do you have any questions?" Answer their questions on the spot. In a five-minute conversation, you can probably address anything and everything they're wondering about. Which means they won't need to bombard you with questions via email, text, or follow-up calls in the future.

Even better, anticipate the top questions they might have ("I know you're probably wondering about XYZ...") and provide answers.

When you do this, your clients will feel seen, heard, appreciated, and cared for. They will relax and know, "Wow, you've thought of everything!" By reaching out personally, you can easily and peacefully transition each existing client to your new pricing.

NOTIFY YOUR EASY CLIENTS FIRST

You're ready to notify your existing clients. So where to begin? Do you start with A (Alicia, Anne, Alex...) and work your way down your client contact list, A to Z, notifying each person one by one?

You could do that. But what I recommend instead is that you start with your *easy clients*.

You know who I'm talking about. The easy clients are the people who absolutely love you, respect you fully, and want to support you and your business in any way possible. They pay their invoices on time, without complaint, and never cause financial drama in your life. These are the clients who bring nothing but good vibes, who continually say, "You're the best!" and even remember your birthday each year. These clients are a sheer delight and aren't intimidating.

Out of all your existing clients, make a list of the easy clients—and notify those people first. Most likely, these easy clients will respond and say:

"Sounds great. Thanks for letting me know!"

"No problem! Appreciate the heads up!"

"You're changing your prices? YAY! It's about damn time. I'm proud of you."

This will boost your confidence and give you the courage you need to speak with your less-easy clients.

Let's recap. By now:

- You communicated your new pricing to new clients.
- You got your team fully on board with the new pricing.
- You did role-playing and sales training so that your team can confidently sell, sell, sell.
- You updated your website, social media profiles, brochures, flyers, and other marketing materials to reflect the new pricing.
- You double-checked to make sure you've deactivated those old payment links and new payments links are working.
- You reached out personally (no mass communication!) to your existing clients to announce the change—specifically, you reached out to your easy clients (the people you know are going to respond positively and won't cause a headache for you).

Now you are ready to notify your less-easy or difficult clients.

Who are these people? Oh. You know who they are.

These are the existing clients who are intimidating, demanding, or question your professional expertise. These also might be clients who haggle, ask for discounts, pay late, or cause financial disruption of some kind or another. These clients might be very perfectionistic—they never accept your work as-is, they always have a million questions and ask you to make a billion tweaks, and yet they're still never satisfied. They might be a wonderful person in many ways! But, for whatever reason, they're a difficult client, and they are not easygoing or flexible. Hopefully, you don't have too many difficult clients.

> *Sidebar: Sometimes, a client who you think will be the easiest actually turns out to be difficult when it comes to pricing changes. It's shocking and rattles you. The same is true in reverse! Someone you perceive as difficult may turn out to be super easy. You just never know until you have the conversation. But, most of the time, your gut is spot-on about who's going to be easy versus tricky.*

Make a list of your difficult people. These will be the very last people you notify about the changes. Because, by the time you contact these people, you want to feel 100% confident. You've already practiced discussing your new pricing with numerous people, you're smooth, you're solid, and you're ready to speak with someone who's a bit more difficult than the others.

When these difficult clients push back and object to your new pricing (which you already suspect they will), you are unwavering. You won't be shaken. You've already heard their concerns, objections, and complaints several times from other, easier clients—and you've got answers prepared in advance. You won't stumble over your words when you respond.

If a difficult client says (in a patronizing tone), "Honey, I'm saying this because I care about you. These prices are too high. Nobody is going to pay these rates."

You can reply and say, "I appreciate your concern. However, these prices have actually been in effect for the last two months. All my new clients—and most of my existing clients—have already transitioned to these new prices. It's been a very smooth transition."

If a difficult client says (sounding huffy and annoyed), "Well, this new pricing won't work for me."

Say, "I'm sorry to hear that because I appreciate having you as a client. I wish you all the best. I hope you can find another service provider who fits what you need. If you ever decide to come work with me again, I'll be here!"

You can calmly let this difficult client go. Farewell. Adiós. Adieu. Auf wiedersehen! When they leave, you will have less stress and more space in your calendar—ready to welcome a brand-new client who will happily pay your new prices.

Remember my client Debbie? When she rolled out her new pricing, she lost 20 clients. Despite losing those 20 clients, her business was still making *more money* each month thanks to her new pricing model. Plus, the 20 clients who left were (you guessed it) her most difficult clients. Debbie wasn't exactly heartbroken to see them leave. In fact, it made her feel 10,000 pounds lighter emotionally. It felt like a joyous holiday gift! Now Debbie's studio is filled with her dream clients, who are all paying her new prices and filling her business with positivity.

DO A GRADUAL ROLLOUT

You might feel motivated to roll out your new prices as quickly as possible. "Rip off the Band-Aid and get it done!" you think to yourself. "Let's do this today!"

But I would caution you against doing this too quickly. In my experience, it's better to roll out your new prices slowly and correctly—rather than quickly and haphazardly. Slow and steady wins the race.

Depending on the size of your business and how many existing clients you have, the complete transition could take anywhere from one to six months. If you're a solopreneur and you only have five or six existing clients, the new pricing rollout will be pretty quick. If you run a larger company with hundreds of existing clients sitting on old, unused prepaid packages, things will take longer.

When I rolled out the new prices at my Pilates studio, it took me three months to make my way through my easy client list—which consisted of roughly 80% of my clients. Around month three, I began working through my difficult client list—the remaining 20%. By month six, I had transitioned 95% of my 156 clients to the new pricing. I only lost three clients in the process.

Your timeline might be different, of course. Maybe you're a virtual assistant, and you have six existing clients. Well, you can probably have a personal conversation with each client to discuss your new pricing this month. It doesn't necessarily need to take six months in your case! But if you run a busy med spa with 500 clients in your database, things may take longer, and that's completely okay.

When you're reaching out to an existing client to notify them about the changes, here's some good language you can use to start the conversation:

"Hey! Thank you so much for purchasing a 20 pack of classes. You have two classes remaining in your pack, which means it's time to re-up soon. We're no longer offering the 20 pack as we did in the past. Instead, we have a new menu of services, and I'd love to walk you through the options...".

"It's been such a joy to work with you. Your package is coming to an end soon. But we can continue working together. I'd recommend the *Maintenance Plan,* which includes [things] for [price] per month. Here's more info on that...."

"I wanted to share some exciting news. To celebrate our fifth business anniversary, we have...a new menu of services! Upgrades all around! Here's what we're offering now...."

The bottom line: Rolling out your new pricing might take some time, and that's just fine. Like crafting a fine wine, you want to take it slow and do it right, building up your confidence as you go. New clients. Then easy clients. Then difficult clients. That's what I recommend.

The timing of your rollout also depends on where you're starting and where you're going. If you're starting this journey with a negative profit margin of -20%, then leaping instantly to pricing that provides a 30% profit margin might be way too big of a leap for you (or your clients) to handle. It may be wiser to do a gradual step-up plan to build up to that 30% mark over time. Your first goal is to reach a break-even number. Then 5% profit, then 10%, and so on. You can offer your long-time clients the option to remain at your old pricing for a short time before getting onto the step-up plan. This is sometimes called "grandfathering" clients at an old rate. However, avoid using this term because it actually has roots in slavery. Instead of saying, "I can grandfather you in..." say, "I can keep you on the old payment option until [date], when we'll need to transition you over to the new plan."

Ultimately, you're the boss. Do whatever rollout strategy—and timing—feels right to you.

If you say, "I want to notify my difficult clients FIRST (not last) and get it over with," okay! If that's what your gut says, go for it.

Or you might say, "I have 1,500 existing customers, and notifying each person, individually, would take me FOREVER. I will be in the grave before it's done! Instead, I'm going to invite all existing customers to join me on Zoom for a special presentation—and I'll announce the new pricing there in an exciting, celebratory way."

Cool! If that's the right approach for you and your clientele, more power to you.

Choose whatever strategy feels best and most authentic for you. In this chapter, my goal is to lay out a variety of options and possibilities—and then it's up to you to confirm the plan that feels right.

WHAT TO SAY?

Throughout this chapter, I've shared brief phrases that you can say to your clients to get them on board with your new pricing. But let's go deeper into "what to say" because this is such a crucial piece of your rollout plan.

I personally believe that honesty is the best policy. This goes for everything in life. As I tell my kids, "The only way out of trouble is to tell the truth. If you are lying, you will be in even more trouble." So if you want to stay out of trouble during your rollout, be honest!

If clients ask, "Why are the prices changing?" you can let them know exactly why. You don't have to break down sobbing or wring your hands apologetically. Just state the honest facts.

Say:

"I crunched the numbers. Unfortunately, if I remain at my 'old' pricing, then my business is headed for trouble—it's not a sustainable model. I need to change my pricing in order to pay my team and myself and generate a profit."

Or say:

"During the pandemic, my business suffered a great deal. We're still recovering.

I need to increase my prices to get us back to a healthy place and be able to pay my team what they deserve."

Or:

"The reality is, I haven't increased my prices since 2009, and this change is long overdue. I need to change my pricing to keep up with inflation and to provide a secure life for myself and my family."

You can be as brutally honest as you want, whatever degree is comfortable for you. You could say:

"Between you and me, this business is one bad month away from closing down. And the reason is our pricing. I've been reluctant to increase prices for a long time because I was scared of how people would react. But I've realized this is something I must do, and I can't put it off any longer. I want this business to survive for a long time, and I want to keep serving clients for many years to come! But to do that, I have to overhaul our pricing. It's not really a 'choice.' It's a must-do."

Whatever the reason, be honest. Clients will respect and appreciate your candor.

When I rolled out the new prices at my studio, which averaged a 35% increase, I was honest about why! Some might even say that I was *too* honest, but I felt that it was the best policy for me and my business.

I told clients:

"I've owned this studio for five years, and I have loved every minute of it. And thanks to clients like you who have been here since the very beginning, I have made it this far. But I have made a lot of mistakes in my business, and the biggest mistake I have made is with pricing. Instead of doing the math to determine exactly how much I should have been charging, I just copied every other studio, and I have been undercharging for years. Five years later, the studio is surviving month-to-month, and I am struggling to keep up. My doctors actually believe that the stress of trying to keep the studio afloat contributed to me contracting meningitis. I finally decided to do the math I should've done on Day 1, and these are the prices I must charge in order for the studio to be sustainable."

Talk about being vulnerable! This was one of the scariest conversations I ever had, and I did it on repeat with 156 clients! But it was the truth. There was no sugar-coating the reality. And, because I had spent the last five years building great relationships with my clients, they all (well, with the exception of three people) totally understood my need to raise my rates. There were very few complaints.

Sure, there were lots of questions about the new pricing options—but these were simply questions, not objections.

Let me repeat that again: *Questions are not objections.*

When clients ask questions about your new pricing, they are not necessarily saying "no"—they're simply trying to understand "what do I get for my money" and "how does this new pricing apply to me, specifically." They are trying to figure out, in their minds, how the new pricing options will fit into their budget, schedule, and routine.

Once you've answered their questions, the majority of your existing clients will say, "Cool. Let's proceed!"

ROLL INTO YOUR FUTURE

You are not just rolling out new pricing. You are rolling into your new and better future. Rollin' into a life where you can take 10 weeks of vacation each year, generate a profit consistently, pad your bank account with savings, and finally have the financial peace and security you've been chasing for so long.

Your rollout plan might take one month to complete successfully (or three months or six). Take your time and do things right.

You may retain all of your clients or lose a few clients along the way. But even if you lose a few people, you will be making more money than before!

Blast the song "Roll Out" by Ludacris (or whatever song makes you feel powerful and energized!) and start mapping out your rollout plan. The sooner you begin, the sooner you'll be running your dream business. 30% profit margin, here we come!

Part Two: Summary

Now that you've reached the end of *Part Two: Overhaul Your Pricing,* let's do a quick recap.

More than anything else, this is what I want you to know:

- My friend, you need to do a profit analysis. I know it might feel uncomfortable and the numbers might be distressing to see. But this is Step One. You have to know where you're starting to figure out where you're going.

- If you do a profit analysis and discover that your profit margin is very tiny, nonexistent, or worse, you actually have a negative profit margin and you're losing money every month, this can be a harrowing moment. You might feel tempted to shut down your business altogether, crawl into a hole, and hide forever. Please don't do that. The current numbers might suck, but these numbers do not spell out where you are going. Only where you are beginning. You can eventually build up to your goal: a profit margin of 30% or higher. It may take several months or a year to get there. The timing is different for every woman, but get there you shall!

- You can calculate your operating expenses, payroll expenses, monthly revenue needs, client capacity, and monthly client value using the formulas I provided. While it might feel difficult to do the math (the first time around), eventually, this will become a simple and normal part of your business routine.

- If the math feels hard and confusing, breathe, slow down, and read each chapter again. On the second reading, things might feel easier to grasp.

- If you read a chapter two or three times and are still utterly bewildered or having a mild heart attack, do yourself a favor and hire a Pricing Overhaul® coach by visiting www.PricingOverhaul.com.

Your coach can either do the math for you or they can double-check your work to make sure you've done all the calculations correctly. If you need a coach, get a coach, and get this work done. Period. Hiring a coach is a relatively small investment (all things considered!) that will bring you peace of mind because you'll know that every single equation is correct. Phew.

- Recurring pricing is your bestie. No matter what kind of business you run, you can figure out a recurring pricing model: high-end services for your clients, even better results for every person you serve, and consistent, predictable monthly income for you. Coming up with recurring pricing is fun! This is the moment to flex your creative muscles and figure out, "What would be an absolute dream experience for my clients? What kind of package or plan would they love? How could I provide that?"

- Lastly, it's important to roll out your new pricing thoughtfully. Don't blast out a mass email that says, "Hey everyone, here are my new prices!" and call it a day. Noooo. You want to approach this strategically and gradually. Your rollout plan might take several months. Take your time and do it right—so that you can retain all of your favorite clients while shedding your nightmare clients. Buh-bye.

Powerful Tools

Good news, my friend.

All the formulas I just provided?

The formulas on how to calculate your operating expenses, payroll expenses, profit margin, and more?

You can access those exact same formulas online—*free of charge*—by scanning the following QR code with your phone, tablet, or another device.

Scan that code, and you'll be directed to
a webpage on www.PricingOverhaul.com.

There, you can input numbers into the equations online—which is great if you're someone who prefers to type rather than write things out by hand.

P.S. Again, if you're feeling super overwhelmed right now and this math feels like a gigantic mountain of misery that you'll never be able to climb, help is here. Visit www.PricingOverhaul.com to hire me or another Pricing Over-haul® coach I've personally trained.

A Pricing Overhaul® coach can walk you through the formulas step by step and ensure that you're doing every calculation correctly.

If you don't want to do the math all by yourself, you don't have to. As a busi-nesswoman, it's important to recognize when you need help. Do whatever you need to do to get this work done. If that means hiring a coach, so be it, and there's absolutely nothing wrong with doing so.

PART THREE

Change Your Life

Welcome to Your New Life

You have invested lots of time, energy, and brain power to overhaul your pricing.

You overcame mindset blocks, insecurities, fear, and doubts. You dismantled a lifetime of false narratives. You silenced the naysayers (the loudest critic may have been the one inside your mind). You tackled the math and came out triumphant. Okay, sure, maybe you had a meltdown or two, sobbed into your glass of wine, dabbed your tears, and did your calculations once again to double-check the numbers. But you chugged forward, and you made it. Here you are.

You have completely changed your pricing and your business.

Now it's time to change your life.

EXPECT THE BEST

From this point forward, you will move through the world *differently*.

Because here's the thing. In order to run a thriving business, you need to radiate success, confidence, and excellence. The way you present yourself. The way you walk into a room—your posture when you sit at your desk. The way you text a client or speak on the phone. The way you treat yourself—and the people around you.

Everything you do, from the biggest action down to the smallest detail, must radiate this message:

> *"I am excellent at what I do. I am proud of my work. I offer premium services with premium pricing to match. I reach for the best things in life. I don't settle for anything less."*

Long gone are the days of moving through the world, expecting less. From this day forward, you are a woman who expects *more!* More for yourself. More for your family. More for other women around you.

You must act upon the expectation of *more* in every aspect of your life. This is how you change your life and the lives of those you love.

We've all heard the saying "You become the company you keep." This is especially true after you roll out your new prices. You need to surround yourself with clients, colleagues, and friends who make you feel powerful and capable. And you absolutely need to surround yourself with people who have a healthy attitude about money. If 95% of your friends believe "it's unethical to make more money" or "it's sooooo hard to find clients," guess what? You will be dragged down into the mud by their beliefs.

Everything you want to achieve begins with what you *believe.*

If you believe that "nobody will pay my new prices" or "my services just aren't worth this amount," that is exactly the reality you will construct for yourself. Like I mentioned in a previous chapter, clients can smell fear. If you don't believe in yourself, nobody else will. To attract clients who know that you are worth it, first you must know that you are worth it.

BECOME THE CLIENT YOU WANT TO ATTRACT

As we move into Part Three, here's an interesting question I want you to consider. It's a three-part question.

- Who is your dream client?
- How does your dream client behave?
- Do you behave this way personally?

For instance, maybe you want to attract clients who are punctual and reliable (they always show up on time), generous (they rave about you to their friends and constantly send new business your way), easy to work with, never waste your time, and have a positive attitude about money (they always pay promptly and never haggle or ask for a discount). That's your dream client!

But do *you* currently behave this way?

Are you reliable, generous, and a sheer delight to work with? Do you pay your bills on time? Do you pay the full amount—no whining or asking for special favors? Do you email people to inquire about hiring them—but then you never follow up and leave them hanging—thereby wasting their precious time?

Are you the client who says, "I don't know…" (trailing off into a quiet sigh of uncertainty)? "I need to think about it…" (for 17 months). "Could I cancel and get a refund?" (Groan.)

Are you the "difficult client" on someone else's roster?

Ouch! That's a harsh question to ask yourself. But answer this honestly. An honest answer is required for you to transform into the person you want your clients to be.

Now is the time to become the kind of client that you want to attract. You need to be her—to get hired by her.

Going forward, you will honor the commitments you've made. You will invest in yourself. You will pay on time. You will be a joy to work with.

When I say "change your life," this is what I'm talking about—becoming the kind of person you want to bring into your life. A full client roster—and prosperous business—begins with you.

WOULD *YOU* WORK FOR YOU?

Once, a mentor asked me, "Erin, would you work for you?"

I'd been struggling with staffing at my studio for a long time. It was a vicious cycle. I couldn't keep instructors. My turnover rate was insane and was creating a major bottleneck in my business. After months of trying different hiring tactics, my coach finally asked me that pivotal question. Would you be happy working for you?

The harsh reality was, no, I would not have worked for me. I would have called myself a controlling bitch, walked out, and found another job. I was not easy to work for. Micromanaging. Unrealistic expectations. Only finding fault. I was a nightmare manager. No wonder I couldn't keep instructors! Once I realized that the problem stemmed from me, I was finally able to build and maintain my dream team.

UPLEVEL YOUR WORLD

You did the math to figure out what you must charge. Now it's time to uplevel your world—your services, your behavior, your influence—to align with those new prices.

It all starts by taking a good, hard look at yourself. Cue: Michael Jackson's "Man in the Mirror" blasting in the background.

Think back to the woman you were before you began your Pricing Overhaul® journey.

Think about who you are today. And who you want to become.

The real transformation begins now.

CHAPTER 17:
Uplevel Your Purchases

When was the last time you purchased something purely to invest in *yourself?* To invest in your own education, well-being, or joy?

I'm not talking solely about large investments like a new car, a new home, or a college degree. I'm also talking about simple, everyday investments that, over time, have a huge impact on your quality of life.

If you want to inspire your clients to invest in themselves, then you need to lead by example.

If you want your clients to purchase premium services with a premium price tag, then you need to do the same.

It starts with you.

This does not necessarily mean you need to rush out and purchase a ticket to attend a $15,000 all-inclusive yoga and wellness retreat on a private island in Tahiti if that is not something you can currently afford. However, you can begin to invest in yourself in smaller ways—and it all adds up.

You can purchase the nice toilet paper instead of the budget, scratchy, paper-thin stuff. Get the mid-price dinner entree instead of the cheapest item on the menu. These micro-choices add up. Your quality of life improves. You begin to carry yourself differently in the world—with more poise, power, and confidence. This, in turn, attracts a different caliber of clients to your business.

One nightly ritual of mine is taking an hour-long bath after dinner to be alone and decompress from the day. I know how luxurious this sounds, but my house considers it a necessity. My husband agrees that I am a better wife and mother when I have my nightly bath. Give me a tub full of scented bubbles, a glass of wine, and pump French music through the sound system. Afterward, I descend the stairs like the next incarnation of Mother Teresa, rosy-cheeked, relaxed, and emanating bliss! I'm only slightly exaggerating.

For years, I used Dr. Teal's Epsom salts in my bath. There is nothing wrong with Dr. Teal's. It is perfectly adequate and smells pretty darn good. Those melatonin bath salts soothed me into countless dreamy slumbers. Depending on where you shop, you can purchase a bulk bag of Dr. Teal's for $4.99 to $9.99. It's available at pretty much any major chain pharmacy or grocery store—a small price tag for a large quantity. For a long time, I was perfectly content with my Dr. Teal's routine.

Cut to spring break 2022 (which sounds like the trailer to an episode of *Girls Gone Wild*) when my family and I enjoyed a week in the Blue Ridge Mountains in a delightful cabin with close friends. While window-shopping in the quaint downtown shopping district one afternoon, we stumbled into a woman-owned boutique that sold candles, perfume, and bath products. The aroma was intoxicating. With all due respect to Dr. Teal's, the fragrances in this shop were on a completely 'nother level. I had never inhaled such luscious, divine aromas before!

After spending a solid half-hour sniffing candles and sampling lotions and experiencing a state of euphoria previously unbeknownst to me, I decided to buy an eight-ounce container of their signature Lime in the Coconut bath salts, which cost $20. Much pricier than my usual Dr. Teal's, but I wanted to give it a try. There was something transformative about these salts. It was like floating on a heavenly cloud while eating key lime pie immediately after the best sex you've ever had—all rolled into one!

Upon returning home, I eagerly anticipated my next bath. I couldn't wait to indulge in a resplendent tub with my new salts. Indulge I did! Every single night. My daughters even got in on the action and loved the Lime in the Coconut fragrance too.

But, woe is me! That tiny eight-ounce container was gone in less than a week—and I found myself craving more.

Normally, I would say to myself, "Ah well, it was nice while it lasted, back to the ol' Dr. Teal's for me!" But this time around, I felt differently.

I thought to myself, "I constantly encourage my clients to uplevel their businesses and their lives. I always tell people to invest in themselves. I need to lead by example and do the same. I need to walk the walk, not just talk the talk!"

Even so, I took a moment of pause. Is it *really* appropriate for me to spend $20 on deluxe bath salts—every week? Is that a *thing* I can do? Is that okay? Who does that??!

But then, I took a step back and looked at the bigger picture. I considered what these bath salts symbolize. And I asked myself, "What is the message I want to send to the world? To my daughters? To my clients? To myself?"

Do I want to send the message, "You don't deserve to have high-end, luxury bath products." "You don't deserve to spend an extra $75 per month on your own happiness." "You only deserve the cheaper, mass-produced product." "You can't afford to shop at beautiful woman-owned small businesses."

HELL NO! That is not the message I want to express through my words, actions, or purchasing decisions.

That's when I decided that I am now officially a Lime in the Coconut woman. On repeat, I made it my duty to order four eight-ounce containers of Lime in the Coconut every month, and I continue to do so to this day.

As I'm sure you've gathered, this story is really not about bath salts. It's about what those salts *represent*. It's about the type of woman you want to be and the message you want to impart to yourself and those around you. It's about *believing* that you deserve nice things—and that others do as well.

After my Lime in the Coconut epiphany, I started evaluating the other items I use on the daily.

The shampoo and conditioner I use to tame my unruly hair (giiiirl, you don't even know. My hair is so thick, I have to shave the bottom half of my hair completely down to the skin for it to be manageable in the South Florida humidity).

The candles I burn at my bedside that energize me in the morning.

The vitamins I give my kids in the morning to keep them healthy and strong.

The sunscreen I spray on their delicate skin.

All of these things, while small and insignificant on their own, contribute to the premium life I want to live. And don't we all want a premium life for ourselves and the people we love?

If you want your clients to buy your high-end, premium services at rates that are higher than your lower-priced competitors, then you must be willing to do the same for yourself—even on something as small as bath salts or sunscreen.

The same goes for the glass of wine you choose at a restaurant. Wouldn't you rather order one glass of Veuve Champagne over three glasses of the house sparkling wine that leaves you with a dull headache the next morning? The organic tea tree oil wipes you use to disinfect the equipment at your gym over the Clorox wipes? The Obagi skincare line you use on your face over Neutrogena? The locally made essential oil diffuser over the Glade plug-ins? The salon quality hair mask over Herbal Essences? Nothing makes me shout "Yes, Yes Yessss!" from the shower more than my Kérastase hair mask from Paris. Let the neighbors wonder, I say!

Don't get me wrong. You don't have to go high-end with every single thing that you buy. A $5 pair of Old Navy flip-flops and a $15 handbag from Target still make me feel like a million bucks. But when you have the desire for something high-end, decide that you are worth it and make the investment in yourself. Allow yourself to indulge in exquisite experiences the same way you ask your clients to do at your business every single day.

I'm not asking you to overextend yourself financially or frivolously buy expensive things unnecessarily. Obviously not. But I'm asking you to *walk the walk*. I'm asking you to know your worth. When something presents itself to you that you truly desire (for me, it's a $350 massage at The Eau Palm Beach Resort & Spa), allow yourself to have this luxury, even if just once and even if there is a cheaper version somewhere else, simply because it enhances your life.

This goes for the services you utilize in your business too. Are you still cleaning your business toilets because you don't want to spend money on a cleaning service? Do you dread updating your QuickBooks file every month because you don't think a bookkeeper's $250 monthly payment is worth it? Are you continuing to "figure it out on your own" because you can't justify the $10,000 enrollment fee to work with a top business coach?

The prosperity of your business begins with whatever is happening inside your own mind.

If you believe "I don't deserve to hire help" or "I'm not going to make much money this year. Therefore, this investment in my business is a waste of money," then your entire business will be built upon a cracked foundation of insecurity and fear.

How you invest in yourself is exactly how your clients will invest too. If you go cheap, they will too. If you go high-end, they will follow. If you're terrified to invest in yourself, well…you get the picture.

I'll never forget after the inaugural Luxury in Business Retreat™ I hosted in Palm Beach, Florida, when an attendee, Christa, had a huge revelation regarding this topic. Christa is a military veteran. After serving one tour in Iraq (she is no stranger to sacrifice), she returned home and opened a yoga studio. There, the sacrifice continued at the expense of her health.

By the time she started working with me to overhaul her business prices, she was physically and emotionally spent. She had been spending every day sacrificing herself for her clients and family and asked nothing in return, not even a paycheck.

Sadly, in addition to running a full-service yoga studio, Christa continued to work a full-time government job because she wasn't making enough at her studio to pay herself. She was an overworked volunteer in her business. She was trapped in a scarcity mindset, scrimping on every single decision and purchase she made for her business, her family, and herself, sacrificing anything she perceived to be a "luxury."

Then she attended my Luxury in Business Retreat™ (after some gentle coaxing from me), which was all about how business owners can and should infuse luxury into their businesses and lives. (If you're interested in attending a Luxury in Business Retreat™, go to www.luxuryinbusinessretreats.com to see the upcoming schedule and locations.)

After one visualization exercise, Christa realized that she had been sacrificing too much, and it was time for her to invest in herself the same way she asked her clients to invest in themselves. It was time for her to *walk the luxury walk*! You want to know the first luxury she decided to invest in for herself? She decided to outsource her family's laundry!

Laundry was the bane of her existence. Mine too. I haven't done laundry since 2015, thanks to our laundry delivery service. The very thought of doing laundry sent Christa into a downward spiral of misery that lasted hours. But there she found herself, week after week, slaving away at her family's laundry for hours on end while her husband and kids were in the other room enjoying quality time with each other. If Christa was one of her clients, she would've told herself to outsource, yet she could never justify the expense for herself.

Finally, it clicked for Christa. "If I expect my clients to buy my services, which could definitely be considered a luxury, then I should expect myself to do the same!" Laundry it was! Christa immediately hired a laundry delivery service upon returning home from the retreat to pick up, wash, iron, and fold her family's laundry, and return it to her doorstep within 24 hours!! Life-fucking-changing!

Sure, Christa could have continued to save $60 per week and done the laundry herself, but the difference between doing her laundry and paying somebody else to do it was life-altering. The same is true for Christa's clients. They could continue to stream free yoga classes online instead of paying for a $199 monthly membership at her studio, but the experience they receive at her studio—and the camaraderie they receive from practicing yoga in the same room with other fellow yogis—is priceless.

Just like Christa, when you choose to invest in yourself and uplevel your quality of life, it creates a magical ripple effect that touches your kids, your home, your business, and the experience your clients receive.

Don't you want your clients to receive the healthiest, happiest version of you—the version of you that is well-rested (not haggard and rundown) and that smells like Lime in the Coconut wafting in the breeze?

Don't you want to move through the world in that way?

Don't you want your clients to treat themselves with that same level of care?

You do, which means you need to lead by example. "Be the Lime in the Coconut that you wish to see in the world!" I am pretty sure Gandhi said that (or something close)!

Here's your luxurious homework assignment:

1. Take a look at the products you use on a daily basis: peanut butter, milk, paper towels, shampoo, and so on. This week, upgrade (at least) one of those items to something high-end. The good stuff. Not the cheap stuff. Begin with one item, for starters. Upgrade to something better and let this be symbolic of a larger shift that's happening in your life.

2. Take yourself out for a meal and buy the item you actually crave, not necessarily the item that is the cheapest.

3. Think about the household chores you currently do every week: dishes, laundry, picking up dog poop from the yard, raking leaves, and so on. Pick one chore you absolutely loathe doing. This week, outsource that dreaded task to someone else. Pay someone to do it! If you feel nervous about doing this, tell yourself, "I'm just going to outsource this chore for one week to see how it feels." Think of it like a one-week gift to yourself. Once you experience how good it feels, you'll be motivated to make this a regular occurrence.

Do those three things this week. I know I am cruelly punishing you by insisting that you buy fancy almond butter and stop doing laundry! You will thank me later.

The bottom line: You can't expect your clients to invest in themselves if you are unwilling to do the same. And you can't expect your clients to say "Yes!" to the high-end, premium services you sell if you're unwilling to give those kinds of experiences to yourself.

And here's the thing: Small investments really *do* make such a difference. If it costs $75 extra to get the fancy bath salts that make you feel like a queen, then you must have those salts and you should accept nothing less. The days of settling for crumbs are over, my friend. A new era has begun for your clients and for you. You are now a Lime in the Coconut woman forevermore.

CHAPTER 18:
Uplevel Your Behavior

Here's the million dollar question:

Would you want you as a client?

If you don't want clients to haggle over pricing, you have to stop doing this.

If you don't want clients to be late paying invoices, you must ensure you always pay on time.

If you don't want clients to cancel their appointments, you need to keep your word and show up with bells.

To uplevel your business and pricing, you need to uplevel your behavior to match. Lead by example. Become a premium service provider who charges premium prices and who conducts herself in a premium way.

You've done the math to calculate the prices you need to charge. Now it's time to consider, "How do I need to *behave?*"

How do you need to shift your behavior to align with your new pricing? This includes your behavior in public *and* your behavior in private. True leadership means doing the right thing even when no one is watching. Take these words to heart. From this moment on, you will conduct yourself in a top-tier manner, no matter where you are or what you are doing.

Decide:

"I will charge high-end prices, and I will support other business owners who do the same."

"I will stop discounting my services and stop expecting others to do the same."

"I will be the client who happily pays full price on the services I utilize."

"I will only work with clients who pay on time, and I will be the client who is always in good standing with payments."

"I will not grumble when fellow service providers increase their prices. In fact, I will congratulate them!"

The way you behave in relation to other businesses is how your clients will behave in relation to yours. It's the simple law of attraction. You get what you give.

The moment I realized this very basic law, everything changed for me and my coaching practice.

"OH SHIT. I'M THE PROBLEM."

In the early years of my coaching business, I often met with business owners who were hesitant to start working with me. After lengthy discovery calls where we would uncover their struggles, pinpoint their desires, and outline how much my services could help them, they knew they needed to work with me. Still, the thought of investing in themselves at that level was terrifying.

Prospective clients often told me, "I really want to do this. I know I need it. But I need to think about it...".

And then I'd never hear from them again. They would "think about it," presumably for the next decade! They felt doubtful about their own abilities as an entrepreneur. They questioned whether or not they would receive a return on their investment, despite literally hundreds of testimonials from previous clients.

"Why do clients keep ghosting me? What exactly is the problem?" I wondered. The answer became clear—and it was not comfortable to confront.

The problem was me.

I realized, "They do this…because I do this too!"

I, too, had attended a handful of discovery calls with other service providers and I provided the same vague and noncommittal responses: "I need to think about it." "I'm in the middle of XYZ project. As soon as I finish, I'll sign up." "I'm waiting on a large payment to come through before I can commit." And so on. Then I vanished without a trace! Poof!

But none of those excuses were true. The truth was, I had never invested in myself and my business at the levels these providers were asking me to, and I doubted myself and whether or not I could make a return on the investment.

Once I stopped making excuses, once I stopped questioning my intuition, and once I started investing in myself and my business at high levels without hesitation, everything changed for my business.

Suddenly, I was attracting clients who acted quickly, didn't make excuses, and trusted themselves to make financial decisions. The new clients I began attracting knew that the investment would pay off because they were unwavering in their belief in themselves and their worthiness. My unwavering trust in myself transferred to the women who then wanted to work with me, and this continues to happen day after day.

Now, in my business, my clients have a collective vision for the future that is so clear that the initial investment to work with me seems like mere pennies! Because it literally is mere pennies after they start making *beaucoup d'argent* (that's "A LOT OF MONEY" for the non-French-speakers out there!) from their new, improved pricing. When you invest in yourself without waffling or hesitation, your clients will be far more likely to do the same.

But sometimes, this lesson doesn't come easily.

I once had a client (whose name I am intentionally withholding) who was religiously late on payments. Every single month, without fail, her autopayments declined. It took days, sometimes weeks, to chase her down to collect payment. Meanwhile, I continued to provide my coaching services to this client despite her payments being in default. Zero consequences were being enforced on my part for late payments, even though I outlined the policy she agreed upon in her contract with me.

With each declined payment came a different excuse.

The client: "I need to transfer money into that account. I'll do it tomorrow."

I thought: "But you know this payment is due on the exact same day of each month. Why didn't you transfer the money ahead of time?"

But I didn't hold her accountable.

The client: "Oops. I need to use a different card."

I thought: "How many cards do you have? You've changed cards five times this year."

Yet I continued to provide my services without complaint.

The client: "I'm waiting on my clients to pay their invoices to me. They're a few weeks late. As soon as they do, I'll have the money and will submit my payment to you."

I thought: "Oh crap! I've been way too lenient with this client when it comes to her payments, and she is also doing the same with her clients. I did not set the right example. Major mentoring fail!"

It was time to hold her accountable.

After one year of consistent late payments from this client, I shared my discovery with her.

"The reality is," I said with trepidation, "your clients consistently pay you late because *you* consistently pay late."

Ouch. That was not an easy truth, especially because I felt partly to blame for setting a poor example.

I allowed this client to continue working with me even when she was late on payments. I accepted her excuses rather than enforcing boundaries. So she, too, did the same with her clients, giving them permission to pay her late while she also continued to service them.

The vicious cycle had to stop, and it had to stop with me! If I wanted the best for this client (which I really did), I had to behave the way I wanted her to behave with her own clients.

I needed to do the same if I expected her to hold her clients accountable to their financial obligations. So I gave the tough love I should've a year prior, and I told her I could no longer continue to coach her unless she began paying on time. I relayed this information with the kindest tone of voice I could muster. I expressed that I truly cared about her, and I wished her every success in the world. However, I would no longer tolerate the previous pattern of behavior.

I'd love to say that my decision to hold this client accountable ended in hugs, kisses, and rainbows, but it did not. In fact, the client decided to part ways with my services, and we haven't communicated since. Major fucking bummer because I loved this client and was so proud of everything she had accomplished in our year working together.

When you uplevel your behavior, some clients will not uplevel theirs. You need to be okay with this. Sometimes, as my dad used to say, "Shit happens and then you die." A lovely, uplifting thought, I know. Well, you will not die. However, you may lose a client or two when you change your behavior. But your behavior as a business owner attracts the same behavior from your clients, and your clients' behavior attracts the same behavior from their clients. If you want better behavior from your clients, you must first change your own.

YOU MUST BECOME YOUR OWN DREAM CLIENT

Despite the loss of my constantly-late-paying client, my business did not suffer. Quite the opposite! My new behavior attracted a new client *the very next day* (I kid you not!) who actually asked me if she could submit her payments *early*! Double-take! Excuse me, what?! "Of course, you can!" I told her. Please and thank you! We have a wonderful experience working together. Fast forward a year or two and now this client wants to become a certified Pricing Overhaul® coach so she can help other women change their businesses and behavior too! None of this would have happened had I continued to enable my former client.

Since then, the number of declined payments I receive each month has dropped to nearly zero. I now attract clients who pay on time and whose clients also pay them on time because I am a person who always pays on time, without fail, and I expect others to do the same.

DO A BEHAVIOR ASSESSMENT

I encourage you to do a self-review (which might be a little painful at first) and consider your typical behavior.

During a normal week or month, how do you conduct yourself?

What behaviors do you notice in yourself that reflect in your clients' behavior?

Cancellations and Refunds

Do you hate when your clients cancel their appointments at the last minute but you frequently do the same?

Do you frequently show up 15 minutes late to appointments, fresh iced coffee in hand, vaguely gesturing about "terrible traffic" en route, putting your hardworking service provider 15 minutes behind schedule for the entire rest of the day, creating a cascading ripple that impacts all future clients on the docket? Well, do you?

Do you register for services or programs then change your mind and send the business owner a lengthy sob story via email about your sick parakeet, your busy schedule, your babysitter canceling, your "financial situation changing," and so forth, and plead for a refund? Thereby burdening her with emotional labor (now she feels obligated to console and comfort you) while simultaneously costing her time and money? Hmm?

Results

Do you get frustrated when clients complain about their results (or lack thereof) even though they're not doing the work but you do the same thing?

Discounts

Do you get annoyed when clients try to negotiate discounts with you but you also ask, "Are you running any special discounts right now" before you purchase something?

Ghosting

Do you throw up your hands in despair when a client monopolizes your time to discuss possibly working together only to ghost you and disappear without even so much as a courteous "no thank you" email? Yet you do this all the time?

Reviews

Does your heart break when a client posts a one-star review about your services ("Why didn't she just say something to me privately instead of posting a public review? I could have addressed this issue and fixed it!")? Yet you routinely post snarky comments online? Or you speak rudely and huffily to customer service representatives who are just trying to help you?

Procrastination

Do you moan internally when clients say, "I just can't afford this right now, hmm, maybe next year" or "I need to think about it…" even though you constantly postpone investments until "someday later" as well?

Bartering

Do you often have clients who come to you with complicated bartering propositions ("Perhaps I could give you a two-hour psychic reading and a Tarot card spread to communicate with your dead cat in exchange for your services") instead of just paying you actual money? Do you often try to barter as well?

Boundaries

Do you have people who try to "pick your brain" for free, people who email you on the weekend and expect an immediate reply, overstep boundaries, or behave inappropriately in other ways? Check your reflection in the mirror.

Look, no one is perfect. We all have areas that require improvement. Acknowledge the parts of your behavior that are in conflict with the woman you want to be and make the commitment to change them!

When you uplevel your behavior, your clients uplevel theirs too. What's more, your confidence shoots through the roof. You feel proud of yourself. You feel rock-solid in your integrity. This, too, takes your business to the next level.

Behave like a high-end, high-earning, high-integrity businesswoman, and that is exactly what you will become—and exactly who you will attract.

CHAPTER 19:
Uplevel Your Influence

Lady, you have evolved!

How good does it feel? Don't you want every single woman to feel this way? To know her worth. To expect more for herself, her family, and her business. To overhaul her pricing. To upgrade the products and services she uses. To uplevel the way she moves through the world.

You must spread this feeling—and knowledge—like wildfire. As an upleveled woman yourself, it is now your responsibility to help other women realize their worth. It is time to influence the women and girls around you.

By overhauling your prices, you give other women permission to overhaul theirs. When a woman decides to open a new business, she will look to you as her pricing role model. She will think to herself, "If that is how much [insert your name here] is charging at her business and she has a ton of happy clients paying those prices, then I can charge those prices too." The old cycle of underearning ends. A new cycle begins.

Most likely, 98% of the women in your industry are undercharging, and *you* have the opportunity to flip your entire industry on its head. You can be the disruptor. The leader in your field. The woman who all other women credit with paving the way.

No matter what industry you work in, you have the power to change it for the better. It only takes one person, and that person is *you!* The decisions you make ripple outward into other women's lives and impact the next generation.

Imagine marching up to a fellow businesswoman you admire and saying:

"With all due respect, you're not charging enough for the incredible value you

provide. I hope you will increase your prices very soon. And I will happily be the first client to pay your newly-increased prices. Sign me up."

Or:

"When was the last time you gave yourself a raise? I encourage you to do it—and I can help you do the math to figure out how much you should be charging. Want me to walk you through it?"

Best of all, picture yourself tucking a crisp $100 bill into the pages of this book and slipping it to a woman you love. Inside, there's a note that says:

"I read this book and followed the steps to overhaul my pricing completely. I urge you to do the same. You deserve to be earning more. Enjoy this book. And because I appreciate your services so much, here's a $100 thank-you bonus. Please treat yourself to something delightful."

Imagine being THAT kind of woman. Imagine the profound influence you would have. Changing lives and bank accounts wherever you go like a Pricing Overhaul® Fairy Godmother!

Can I let you in on a little secret? The more I encourage the women around me to earn more, the more money I make. Encouraging other people to prosper will boomerang right back to you. Seriously. The universe has a funny way of rewarding you for good behavior.

In fact, I love telling service providers, "You should charge me more than you currently do!" Every time I do this, strange magic unfolds in my life. Here's just one example....

"YOU CHARGED ME HOW MUCH?"

It should be no surprise that I love doing my own bookkeeping. Updating my QuickBooks file is the first thing I do every morning while sipping my first cup of coffee. I have done my own bookkeeping for years, which gives me so much joy and allows me to stay on top of my finances every day.

But I used the old QuickBooks Desktop version for years because it was cheaper than the online version. *eye roll* I know. Can you believe I used to operate that way? Shut the fuck up to ME!

As part of my mission to uplevel the services I use, I decided to upgrade from QuickBooks Desktop to QuickBooks Online with its more expensive monthly subscription fee. However, I am a creature of habit. I knew QB Desktop like the back of my hand, and the one thing that gave me pause over making the change was the learning curve involved in learning the new software. So I decided to hire a QuickBooks expert and bookkeeper to help me transfer all of my books to the new QB Online platform and teach me how to use the new version.

I felt my shoulders drop out of my ears and felt such relief knowing, "A pro is going to give me a tutorial and teach me everything I need to know."

The woman I hired, Nichole, was so knowledgeable and helpful, and she made the entire process so easy for me. She was attentive, patient, and dedicated hours of time to ensuring that I felt comfortable with the new platform. She was immensely generous and made the transition process a complete dream!

Then, she submitted her invoice to me and I nearly fell off my chair. The amount she charged me was *shockingly low*. I expected to pay her significantly more than what she charged. This had to be a mistake. When I questioned if the invoice was correct, Nichole said, "Yep. That's it. I didn't really do much."

She didn't really do much?! Was she fucking kidding?! I resisted the urge to tell her to shut the fuck up because she wasn't a client of mine (yet), but I really wanted to.

What seemed effortless and easy to Nichole was a godsend to me. I could not have done it without her. Well, I'll take that back. I could've done it without her, but I didn't want to do it without her! I didn't want to put forth the effort to search through online FAQ boards and help articles to learn how to do it on my own. I wanted to pay an expert, Nichole, to show me the way, save me time, and prevent me from making stupid mistakes.

Although the help Nichole provided seemed like "no big deal" to her, her services provided immense value to me.

That's the thing. Just because what you offer seems like "nothing" to you does not mean that your clients feel the same way.

For instance, I can overhaul a business pricing in under an hour with very little effort. I can do it blindfolded and with my hands tied behind my back (well, not really, I need my eyes and hands to update spreadsheets, but overhauling a business' prices is no biggie for me)! I do it every single day without breaking a sweat. But just because it's a piece of cake for me doesn't mean the same is true for my clients! Prior to hiring me, my clients are stuck in a vicious cycle of undercharging and overworking. After hiring me, they're in a vastly better place: healthy profit margin, dream schedule, feeling badass instead of burnt out. The results I provide are invaluable to my clients, so they are willing to pay every dollar I charge.

The same is true for Nichole. She could've transitioned me to QuickBooks Online in her sleep, but that didn't matter. Just because the task is "easy" for her does not mean it should be "cheap" for me as the client. The expertise she provided to me was invaluable, and she needed to charge more. I couldn't allow her to continue charging pennies for her services.

I was obligated as a pricing expert to tell her that she wasn't charging enough—which is exactly what I did.

I paid her invoice—but I paid *double* what she charged—and I sent her this little note:

"You're not charging enough. You could have easily charged me $500, and I wouldn't have batted an eye. You need to start charging more."

She immediately responded to my email and said, "When the creator of Pricing Overhaul® tells you that you need to increase your prices, you should probably listen. Thank you!"

And increase her prices she did! The next time I requested her help for a payroll issue I was having, she charged me four times what she had originally charged me. Bravo! Can we give Nichole a standing ovation?

Actually, can we start giving standing ovations to every single woman when she increases her rates? Let's start a movement! A movement that encourages women to charge more and congratulates them when they do instead of shaming them. I want every woman who reads this book to tell another woman, "You could be charging a lot more, and I hope you will."

TO INFLUENCE OTHERS, TELL YOUR STORY

This movement starts with an honest conversation about your financial struggles. Tell your story. Talk openly and honestly about money. Proudly share your financial successes with other women and your past mistakes. Tell them how much you make after overhauling your prices. Share this book with them and encourage them to read it.

Imagine if you could inspire your closest friends, your daughters, sister, aunt, mom, and other women who are important to you...to charge more? Imagine how this would change your family lineage, your community, and the world.

Each of those women can continue to expand the ripple to another woman and another. Little girls will grow up seeing that women are badass business owners who make their own money, and lots of it! They will grow up expecting to open their own businesses, expecting to make lots of money, and expecting *more* for themselves in all ways.

I see this happening with my own daughters. As long as they've been alive, they've never known their mom to work for somebody else. Mommy doesn't have a job. Mommy owns businesses. This is all they know. That mommies own businesses and make a lot of money and soak in tubs with Lime in the Coconut luxury bath salts.

Naturally, growing up with this example, they have never talked about what "job" they want to have when they grow up. Instead, they talk about what kind of business they want to own (which brings proud tears to my eyes!).

Just the other night, after I finished writing Chapter 17 of this book, my youngest daughter, Parker (who was seven years old at the time of writing), joined me in my nightly bath. Laying in the bath together, Parker started asking about my book. I explained that my book teaches women who own businesses how to make lots of money and how much they should charge.

Parker's ears perked up. She said, "Mommy, I want to make lots of money. Can you read your book to me?"

"Of course. Do you want to hear the chapter I wrote today?"

For 15 minutes, Parker sat and stared attentively at me while I read the chapter to her. I could tell she was deep in thought. When I finished reading, she stood up in the bathtub—with her cute little, naked booty (moms, you know what I'm talking about)—and she said, "Mommy, I want to write a book! I want to write a book about how to make money for kids. I already have four ideas for four chapters: one, a lemonade stand; two, sell your artwork; three, doggie daycare; four, dog walking."

"That's brilliant, Parker. Yes. You should absolutely write that book!"

With that, she ran her cute little booty out of my bathroom, leaving a trail of bubbles in her wake. After putting on her PJs, she ran downstairs and wrote her book, complete with illustrations from her older sister, Stevie.

When I asked Parker how much she would sell her book for, Stevie blurted out, "Whatever you think you're going to charge, Parker, charge more!"

My heart just about exploded with pride and joy! Two tiny little Pricing Overhaul® experts are born! Running loose in the wild!

I want to normalize women and girls earning *more*. I want prosperity to be the norm rather than struggle. I want to provide an inheritance for my daughters—passing down money, certainly, but also passing down powerful beliefs and convictions.

IT STARTS WITH YOU

You, too, can begin a ripple that touches hundreds or even thousands of lives.

It starts with setting an example for your daughters and encouraging them to think of ways they can make money for themselves.

It starts with you telling your yoga instructor that she isn't charging enough.

It starts with you encouraging your friend who is desperate to leave her job to start her own business.

I have talked countless friends into leaving their miserable, underpaying jobs and going into business for themselves.

One such friend, Sally, had been chatting with me about her idea to open her own pediatric psychology practice for months. Sally is a school psychologist who worked for the public school district in Florida, the third lowest paying state in the country for teacher pay (it's really a sad, pathetic state of affairs), so you can imagine how little she was making. Sally's salary for her skill level just wasn't cutting it. In fact, when we first met—our daughters were in the same class together, so we met when they were both in kindergarten—Sally was making in one year what I was making in one month. To supplement her income, Sally started conducting educational evaluations and counseling services privately as a side hustle.

One night, while waiting for our daughters to perform in their Christmas chorus concert, Sally and I began chatting about careers and money. I was on the brink of my first $50K month, and as she and I were talking, my phone was blowing up with payment notifications from clients. *Ding.* Another payment. *Ding.* Then another.

"Sally, you see my phone blowing up? I just hit $47K in sales this month!"

She was astonished. "$47K...and that's just this month?"

"Yep! And there are still three days left!"

I could see Sally's wheels spinning. "That's how much money I make in an entire year!" she gawked.

"I know. I'm telling you, Sally. You need to quit your job and go into business for yourself! You are an amazing psychologist. You have valuable skills. You could make so much more money than you do right now. And you could be working so much less. Sally, I only worked 18 hours this month, and I'm going to make $50,000."

Just as the words left my mouth, I felt a momentary sting of regret. Did I say too much? Is this TMI? Does this sound like I am boasting about my own success? I paused, waiting to see how Sally would react and hoping I hadn't overshared.

After a beat, Sally replied, "You are so right. I'm going to do this."

Sally knew that her hard-won skills were worth so much more than the scraps she was being paid by the state government. She knew she could increase her income. And she was ready.

She began asking me questions. "What's the first step I should take? How much were you making a year when you first started your coaching practice? What's realistic as I am getting started?"

We talked all night long. When I revealed to her that I made $10,000 a month when I started my coaching business, she was flabbergasted.

"$10,000 a month is how much you made when you *started?*"

"Like I said, Sally. You could be earning so much more than you currently do. Once you quit your job, the floodgates will open, and you'll realize how much more is possible."

Over the next couple of months, our regular Moms' Night Outs turned into business dinners where we talked shop, and I walked her through my Pricing Overhaul® method and business model. She started seeing new possibilities for herself, and over wine and cheese, we discussed ways she could turn her side hustle into her full-time gig.

One afternoon, several months after the night of my big reveal, I received the best text message from her:

"So I just calculated my upcoming evaluations scheduled for this month, and they're projecting that I will make $10,000 in ONE MONTH. My first $10,000 month. I thought you were totally crazy when you threw that number out at the beginning of the year. But that's been my goal ever since you mentioned it. OMG, I did it, and the month is not even over."

I mean, come on. Is there anything better than that?!

When you overhaul your prices and start making the income of your dreams, shout it from the rooftops. Tell other women how much you're making and how you're doing it. It's not enough to uplevel your own income. You need to uplevel your *influence*, too, and touch other women's lives. Share what you've learned. Lift another woman as you rise, because all women deserve *more*.

You are more influential than you might think.

Simply by sharing your story with one person, you can forever change that woman's life.

A better world starts with you. And it starts today.

Part Three: Summary

Now that you've reached the end of *Part Three: Change Your Life*, it's time for a quick recap.

More than anything else, this is what I want you to know:

- Effective immediately: You will no longer settle for peanuts and pennies, scraps and crumbs, or the cheapest bath salts in the bulk-discount-bin at the store!

- From this moment on, you are a woman who expects more. More for yourself. More for your family. More for other women around you.

- However, in order to receive more, you must uplevel your purchases and your behavior.

- Instead of buying the cheapest item, choose the high-end option that you truly want. Instead of haggling for discounts, pay full price and make your payment on-time or early. Instead of canceling at the last minute, keep your word.

- The more you invest in yourself and carry yourself with integrity, the more you'll attract clients who are happy to do the same.

- Lastly, it is not enough to overhaul your own pricing. It's your responsibility to encourage your fellow women to do the same. You can disrupt your industry and change lives simply by sharing what you have learned.

- Encourage a service provider to charge more. Tell a colleague to read this book. Or pay an invoice (but pay double what's being asked) and explain why. One of the most powerful things you can say to a woman is: "You should charge a lot more and I'll be first in line to pay." Hearing this one sentence will change her life.

- Through actions like these, you create a ripple effect that reaches many, many people. We don't need to live in a society where women are overworked, exhausted, and earning piddly piles of nothing. We can do better. And it all starts with you.

Conclusion

My dear reader,

I want you to know that I am proud of you. Incredibly proud.

I know that's a super cheesy mom-thing to say—hello, mom of two here who proudly drives a minivan—but it's true. I am proud of you!

You could have easily picked up this book, flipped through it, realized that it wasn't going to be a leisurely beach read like you originally thought, and tossed the book on top of your pile of unread books...never to look at it again.

But you didn't.

You could have easily read the word "math" at the very beginning of the book and said, "Ah hell naw! I can't do math"...promptly tossing this book into the bin!

But you didn't.

You could have allowed yourself to get overwhelmed by the formulas and math equations.

But you didn't.

You could have allowed yourself to continue to operate your business, charging the same ol' prices that haven't served you.

But you didn't!

Instead, you persisted. You told your inner critic to "shut the fuck up" numerous times. You challenged false beliefs about yourself. You rewrote old narratives. You faced very real mindset blocks and kicked them to the curb. You did the fucking math—yes, I realize I've used the word "fuck" a lot in this book, but dammit, it's such a powerful word. And a random little fact here is that the word "fuck" is one of only a few words in the English language that can be used as a noun, verb, adverb, and adjective. It's like the superwoman of words! There's nothing it can't do!

You calculated how much you should actually be charging to live the life of your dreams, and you fucking rolled out new prices. Like what?! You did that!

Most importantly, you made it out the other side stronger, wiser, and wealthier! You are a living testimonial to the power of belief in one's self and the power of math.

You know you are worthy of this change, and you stand unwavering in this knowing.

You know that EVERY SINGLE WOMAN is worthy of more too, and you preach it from the mountaintops.

I'll say it again: I am proud of you.

Seeing as how I am a mom, I'm going to end this book with a story about my daughters. Since the day my daughters were born, I put them to bed with the following mantra. This mantra is so ingrained in our lives that I even have it tattooed on my shoulder blade. The mantra goes:

You are KIND.
You are SMART.
You are STRONG.
You are BRAVE.

They have heard this mantra every single day of their lives, and it's baked into their DNA. Now at bedtime, all I say is "You are," and they complete the sentences on their own.

Me: "You are?"

My daughters: "Kind."

Me: "You are?"
My daughters: "Smart."

Me: "You are?"
My daughters: "Strong."

Me: "You are?"
My daughters: "Brave."

I share this with you because by overhauling your prices, you are being KIND to yourself.

By overhauling your prices, you are making SMART decisions that will change the trajectory of your business and life.

By overhauling your prices, you are being STRONG even if you feel nervous and scared to make the changes you must make.

By overhauling your prices, you are being BRAVE because YOU are leading the way for other women.

Congratu-fucking-lations!

Please go forth and enjoy your new-and-improved business, new pricing, and new life.

And if you ever find yourself in Florida, you'll find me at the swanky tapas bar or lounging by the pool, and you can saunter over and tell me, "Erin, I did the math, I overhauled my pricing, and now I'm earning way more than be-fore." And if you want to purchase a round of premium top-shelf margaritas to celebrate together, my friend, I will not protest!

To your new, prosperous, and beautiful life....

-Erin

Pricing Overhaul® Resources

If you enjoyed this book and want to continue learning from me, visit www. PricingOverhaul.com.

Here are a few resources on the site I encourage you to check out.

COURSES

I offer several courses you can take conveniently online. Study from wherever you are. Including:

- Cash Management 101
- Financial Check-Up
- Raise Rates Without Losing Clients
- How Much is My Business Worth
- How to Price Profitable Retreats That Sell Out
- And more

By enrolling in a course, you can access my private support group (for clients only), where you can ask questions and get personalized help.

You can also become a member of Once Upon a Profit, which gives you access to ALL of my recorded courses plus all live masterclasses as long as you're an active member.

Get all the details at:

https://pricingoverhaul.com/online-courses/

RETREATS

Attend a Luxury in Business Retreat™. Otherwise known as the best week of your entire life.

Expand your mind and your business…while savoring gourmet food, sipping local wine and spirits, and strolling through exotic locations across the globe. Did I mention the ability to write off a vacation as a business expense?

https://luxuryinbusinessretreats.com

COMMUNITY

Visit the Pricing Overhaul® Facebook group to meet fellow women in business and to discuss all things related to money, biz, pricing, mindset, and more.

https://www.facebook.com/groups/pricingoverhaul

INSPIRING STORIES

Read client success stories and get inspired by the big leaps these women have made.

https://pricingoverhaul.com/client-testimonials/

EXPERT COACHES

Meet Pricing Overhaul® coaches I've trained in my methodology. These coaches are fully qualified to work with you one-on-one, take you by the hand, guide you through all the math, and help you overhaul your business and pricing.

If you want someone to help you "do the math," these coaches can walk you through it and do the calculations for you while still ensuring that you understand each step and feel empowered along the way.

https://pricingoverhaul.com/

INSPIRATION AND FUN

Follow me on Instagram at @pricingoverhaul if you'd like to see photos of my latest family vacation, post-workout selfies, and tips on pricing, business, and more.

You can also find me on Facebook at:

https://www.facebook.com/pricingoverhaul

Additional Resources

In addition to the copious resources at www.PricingOverhaul.com, here are some additional resources I highly recommend.

These books and podcasts have made a difference in my life and the lives of my clients.

BOOKS

Whenever a client asks, "Can you recommend a good book on money that I should read?" I always recommend:

We Should All Be Millionaires by Rachel Rodgers
Rich As Fuck by Amanda Frances
The Law of Attraction by Esther Hicks and Jerry Hicks
A Happy Pocket Full of Money by David Cameron Gikandi
Think and Grow Rich by Napoleon Hill

P.S. Confession: I rarely read actual books because I prefer audiobooks instead! All the books I just mentioned are available in audio format too.

PODCASTS

Here are some of my favorite podcasts on business, money, mindset, and more:

HBR Ideacast
Abraham Hicks Daily
She Makes Bank

The Gifted Woman with J Muenz
Let's Make Work Human
News in Slow French
Coffee Break French (just because I am a French-enthusiast and love learning the language)

Hire a Pricing Overhaul® Coach

By reading this book, you learned exactly how to overhaul your pricing. You've got the formulas. You are perfectly capable of doing the math—on your own. And you can. (Remember the beginning of this book? You are good at math!)

That said, just because you can do something all by yourself doesn't necessarily mean you want to. It can be very helpful to work with a trained coach who can guide you step by step.

If you're feeling a bit overwhelmed and want to hire a pro, help is here.

Visit https://pricingoverhaul.com/ to hire a Certified Pricing Overhaul® Coach. You can work with a coach I have personally trained in my methodology or with me.

You'll work one-on-one with your coach. We have virtual options (Zoom, Voxer, email, etc.), so we can get everything done together online. You don't even need to leave your office or home.

Your Pricing Overhaul® coach can:

- Input numbers into the correct formulas
- Calculate your profit margin, operating expenses, monthly client value, and more
- Do the math for you (or double-check your work to make sure everything is correct)
- Help you figure out exactly what you must charge
- Brainstorm with you to figure out recurring revenue options for your business
- Answer your pricing questions, large and small

- Hold space for you compassionately if you feel fearful about changing your existing pricing model
- Help you figure out an excellent rollout plan to announce your new pricing
- And very lovingly tell your inner critic to shut the fuck up

Does this sound like exactly what you need?

Go book a session with your dream coach.

Having a coach can make all the difference in the world.

Become a Pricing Overhaul® Coach

Is this you?

- You would love to help women business owners overhaul their pricing and make considerably more money.
- You love helping clients shift from "overwhelmed" to "competent, successful, and confident."
- You have a natural aptitude for numbers and love checklists, spreadsheets, and formulas (or you're willing to learn!)
- You have an encouraging personality. "Yes you can!", "You got this!", and "Totally doable!" are things you think and say all the time.
- You'd like to start a side hustle to make extra money as a Pricing Overhaul® coach.
- You could see yourself doing coaching full time.
- Or you already work in a coaching or business/finance-related profession (business coach, bookkeeper, accountant, tax preparer, financial planner, etc.) and you'd like to add a new credential to your resume.

If that's you, you'd be an excellent Pricing Overhaul® coach.

Enroll in my Pricing Overhaul® coach certification program.

Let's begin your training. You could be working with clients (changing businesses and lives) in as little as 12 weeks.

https://pricingoverhaul.com/

Coaching is such a rewarding profession. It feels incredible to get texts and emails from clients saying, "I did it!", "I raised my prices!", "I just had my highest-earning month of all time!", and, "It's thanks to you."

Acknowledgments

Can I share a secret?

Many people say, "Writing a book is exhausting…" or "It took me 20 years to painstakingly peck out this manuscript, and it is drenched with my blood, sweat, and tears…", but I gotta be honest, that wasn't my experience. The truth is, I wrote this entire book in less than six weeks, and it was actually so much fun!

I wrote the book in short bursts while soaking in the tub (I have a little wooden stand where I propped up my laptop), lounging outside in the backyard, in sushi restaurants and wine bars, and even sitting in the van while parked outside waiting for my girls to finish gymnastics class. I wrote several chapters at a high-end spa—in a post-massage haze of bliss—which was one of the best days of my whole year. Writing this book felt like a dream come true, not a chore.

So it would be deceitful to say that "writing this book was soooo hard" because it honestly was not. It was a joy. I've wanted to share these Pricing Overhaul® methodologies in a book format for many years, and the words poured out rapidly. This book just wanted to be born.

That said, writing a book is definitely a team effort. Several people supported me with their encouragement, helpful suggestions, or by graciously allowing me to include their stories.

I want to take a moment to thank:

First and foremost, my husband, Eric, who supports me 100% every single time I say, "I have an idea."

My daughters, Stevie and Parker, who teach me what's most important in life.

My energy coach, J Muenz, for helping me activate my gifts and share them with the world.

My executive coach and spiritual advisor, Emma Churchman, for guiding me to always make decisions in alignment with my true desires.

All of my clients who have trusted me and allowed me to share their stories.

My girlfriends who cheered me on the entire way (you know who you are).

Last but not least, Alexandra Franzen, my book coach, who made this process so easy!

To everyone who played a role in making this book possible: *thank you.*

About the Author

Erin B. Haag is the founder of Pricing Overhaul®, a company that teaches self-employed women how to overhaul their pricing and make more money than they ever dreamed possible.

Prior to starting the Pricing Overhaul®, Erin founded a successful Pilates and yoga studio in Palm Beach, Florida—which she ran for several years before selling the company for 40x her original investment.

Erin brings 20 years of experience to her clients. From calculating your revenue, expenses, owner's salary, profit margin, and beyond, Erin loves crunching the numbers to determine exactly what you need to charge. Her motto is "trust the math," because the numbers never lie.

Before becoming an entrepreneur, Erin worked for several top businesses in the health, wellness, spa, and beauty industries. Her resume includes area supervisor for LA Weight Loss, call center manager for Ideal Image, corporate sales trainer for SLEEK Medspa & Surgical, QVC spokeswoman for Britesmile, and regional director and teacher trainer for Power Pilates. Working for these multimillion-dollar brands taught Erin what to do (and what not to do) if you want to run a profitable business, and she passes along her knowledge to each client she serves.

When she's not working, Erin loves soaking in her bathtub, attending French lessons, and planning her next family vacation. She lives in Florida with her husband, two daughters, and golden retriever, Lulu.

Erin is available for speaking engagements, media appearances, and margaritas. Visit www.PricingOverhaul.com to stay connected with Erin and explore her courses and services.

References

Cantlon, Jessica. 2019. "Gender similarities in the brain during mathematics development." Science of Learning. 4:19. November 2019. https://doi.org/10.1038/s41539-019-0057-x

Klara, Robert. "Throwback Thursday: When Doctors Prescribed 'Healthy' Cigarette Brands." Adweek. June 18, 2015. https://www.adweek.com/brand-marketing/throwback-thursday-when-doctors-prescribed-healthy-cigarette-brands-165404/

Fidelity Investments, 2021 Women and Investing Study (Smithfield: Fidelity Investments, 2021).

Lipscomb, Sam. 2021. "Women Outperform Men in Investing: Here's Why." Yahoo. October 11, 2021. https://www.yahoo.com/video/women-outperform-men-investing-why-204459350.html

Reilly, David. 2022. "Men think they're brighter than they are and women underestimate their IQ. Why?" The Conversation. March 14, 2022. https://theconversation.com/men-think-theyre-brighter-than-they-are-and-women-underestimate-their-iq-why-178645

Spencer, Steven. 1999. "Stereotype Threat and Women's Math Performance." Journal of Experimental Social Psychology Volume 35, Issue 1. January 1999. 4-28.

Gross, Jenny. 2020. "Wealthy Millennial Women Tend to Defer to Husbands on Investing." New York Times. October 24, 2020. https://www.nytimes.com/2020/10/24/business/millennial-personal-finance.html

Werber, Cassie. 2019. "Wealthy millennial women are more likely to defer to their husbands on investing." Quartz at Work. March 15, 2019. https://qz.com/work/1573457/wealthy-millennial-women-are-deferring-to-their-husbands-on-financial-planning/

WBENC. n.d. "Behind the Numbers: The State of Women-Owned Businesses in 2018." Accessed September 9, 2022. https://www.wbenc.org/news/behind-the-numbers-the-state-of-women-owned-businesses-in-2018/

Beauty. 2017. "9 Times Dolly Parton Proved the Higher the Hair, the Closer to Heaven." Vogue. September 22, 2017. https://www.vogue.com/slideshow/dolly-parton-big-hair-blonde-curls-bobs-beehives-beauty-9-to-5-country-western-singer-gallery

Aklap, Nellie. 2015. "Survivng Your First Year As A Small Business Owner." Forbes. May, 11, 2015. https://www.forbes.com/sites/allbusiness/2015/05/11/surviving-first-year-as-small-business-owner/?sh=13aab6c78e55

Printed in the USA
CPSIA information can be obtained
at www.ICGtesting.com
LVHW040932010524
778877LV00001B/67